Getting Around in

Glacier National Park

Mike Butler

America Through Time®
ADDING COLOR TO AMERICAN HISTORY

America Through Time is an imprint of Fonthill Media LLC
www.through-time.com
office@through-time.com

Published by Arcadia Publishing by arrangement with Fonthill Media LLC
For all general information, please contact Arcadia Publishing:
Telephone: 843-853-2070
Fax: 843-853-0044
E-mail: sales@arcadiapublishing.com
For customer service and orders:
Toll-Free 1-888-313-2665

www.arcadiapublishing.com

First published 2021

ISBN 978-1-63499-292-3

Typeset in 10pt on 13pt Sabon
Printed and bound in England

ACKNOWLEDGMENTS

I will always be grateful to my parents, Ray and Marian Butler, for taking me and my brother on our first camping trip to Glacier National Park in 1969. There have been many trips to Glacier since then, but it was that very first trip that began my life-long love of the park and its geography and history.

I would like to thank my brother, Dr. David Butler, for his loan of books from his personal library for research for this project, as well as for the loan of one of the photographs in this book. Thanks also for his willingness to answer my questions, for proofreading this text, and for his companionship on several trips to Glacier National Park. Thanks also go to Ian B. Tippet, longtime personnel manager for Glacier Park Inc., who passed away in 2020. Without Mr. Tippet hiring me to be a red bus driver in 1972 and 1973, this book would never have materialized.

Historic photographs in the book come primarily from the collection of the Glacier National Park archives. They are annotated as "NPS GLAC." Other photographs from the National Park Service are annotated simply "NPS." Some photographs come from the Library of Congress and the Oregon Historical Society Library. They are annotated as such. I am deeply indebted to the early pioneer photographers of Glacier whose images appear in this book.

Wallace Stegner wrote in his 1965 introduction to A. B. Guthrie's classic mountain-man novel *The Big Sky*, "Geography, at least, is one matter in which a Westerner can excel and in which he takes pride. History is another." As a Westerner myself, my hope is that this book aptly reflects those sentiments.

While researching this book, I consulted many sources (see Bibliography). However, any resulting errors in the text are strictly my own.

Contents

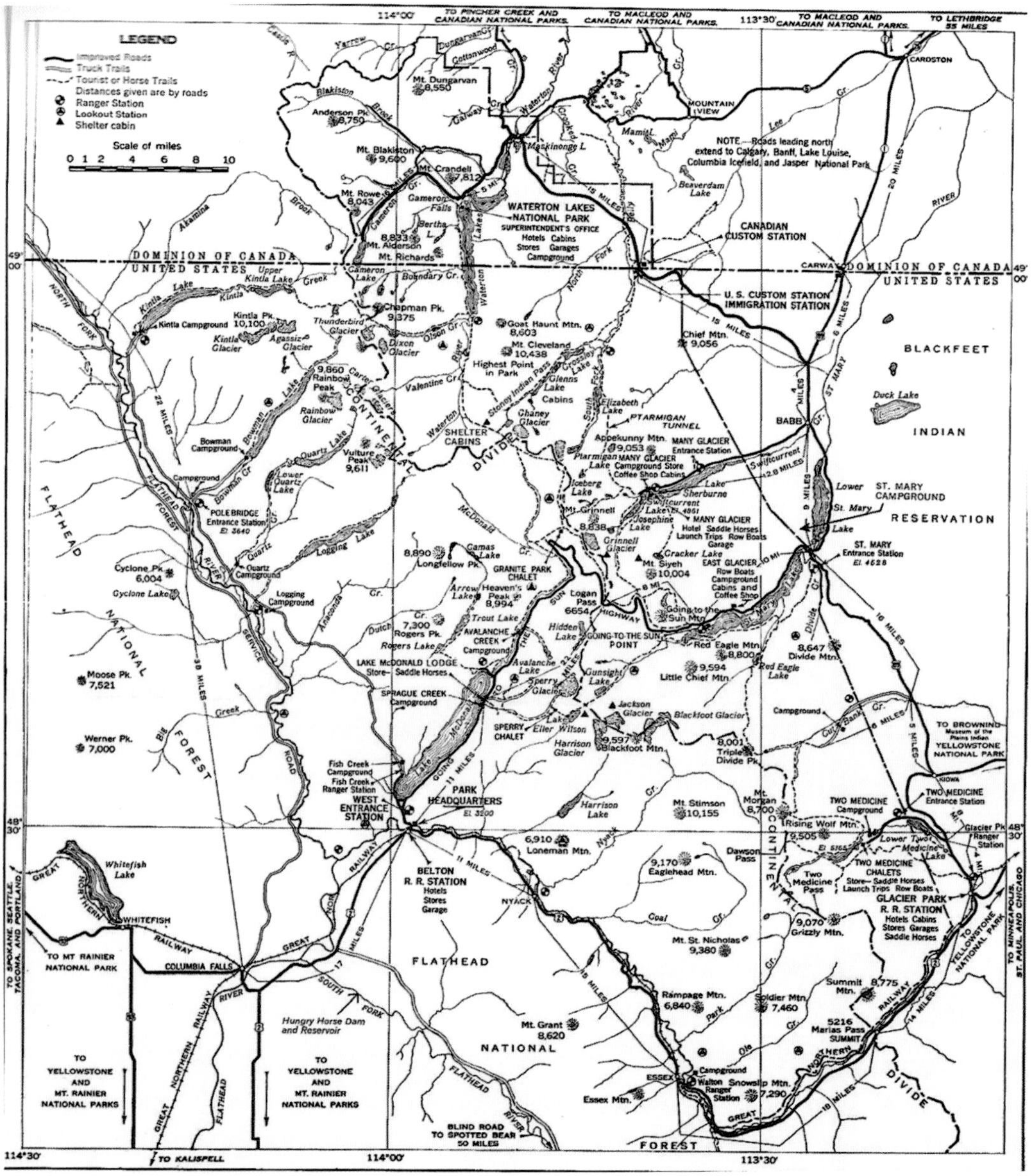

Map of Glacier National Park, *c*. 1940s.

INTRODUCTION

"FOR THE BENEFIT AND ENJOYMENT OF THE PEOPLE"

When Glacier became a national park in 1910, the only access to the park was the Great Northern Railway, which stopped at Midvale (East Glacier) and Belton (West Glacier). The only road in the park, between Belton and Apgar, at the foot of Lake McDonald, was a 3-mile stretch of "quagmire, corduroy, and misery, dreaded by those who had ridden over it, (and) feared by those who expected to."[1] The road had first been constructed by settlers at Lake McDonald and residents of Belton in 1895, and it has seen little improvement since. Development of transportation systems within the park thus became the highest priority for newly appointed Superintendent William R. Logan in 1910. In fact, his official title was "Superintendent of Road and Trail Construction." However, construction was seriously delayed by the extensive forest fires of 1910. The purpose of this book is to trace the development of transportation systems within Glacier National Park and to explain how those systems created the structures and roads seen in the park today.

President William Howard Taft signed the legislation creating Glacier National Park on May 11, 1910, thirty-eight years after the creation of America's first national park, Yellowstone, in 1872. Americans realized that the frontier West, as they knew it, was coming to a close in the late 1800s, and they feared that the spectacular landscapes of the West would be spoiled by development unless set aside and preserved for future generations. Deirdre Shaw, museum curator of Glacier, stated:

> By the late 1890s ... the perceived end of the western frontier triggered a concern among some Americans that the wildness of places like Glacier would soon be gone. The resulting movement sparked the creation of national parks ... which seek to preserve a bit of the pristine frontier for future generations.[2]

The creation of the national parks developed a conflict between preservation and use that still rages today. The very act that created Yellowstone National Park in 1872 called for "the creation of a public park or pleasuring ground for the benefit and enjoyment of the people."[3] Furthermore, "the Organic Act of 1916 established the National Park Service and required that national parks, monuments, and reservations be preserved 'unimpaired for the enjoyment of future generations.'"[4] Thus the enacting legislation for the national parks and the National Park Service established the two-fold purpose of preservation of the land and enjoyment (use) of the people. How to balance these two principles has always been a challenge for the National Park Service, and the conflict played out in the development of transportation and facilities in Glacier National Park. Where should roads be built in the park? Should hotels be built in the park or outside of park boundaries?

Initially, in Glacier, the development argument carried the day. Glacier was virtually a pristine wilderness, with only a few private cabins on the shores of Lake McDonald and the remains of mining claims in the Many Glacier valley. However, the Great Northern Railway ran along Glacier's southern boundary, and its founder James J. Hill "intended to develop Glacier as the 'playground of the Northwest:'"

> [He intended to] make it fully competitive with attractions advertised by his competitors, the Canadian Pacific and Northern Pacific Railways, (and the Great Northern) began planning and constructing facilities near and in Glacier as soon as President Taft signed the park bill.[5]

Thus, the Great Northern Railway completed construction of the Belton Chalet in the summer of 1910. In 1912, James J. Hill's son, Louis Hill, purchased 160 acres of land on the Blackfeet Reservation at Midvale and began construction of Glacier Park Lodge, which was completed in 1913 at a cost of $500,000. Also in 1913, "the railroad continued its construction of trails, 'tepee camps,' and chalets within the park itself."[6] In 1915, the Great Northern Railway completed another project within the park's boundary—the massive Many Glacier Hotel on the shore of Lake McDermott (later renamed Swiftcurrent Lake). The Great Northern was certainly doing its part in creating a "pleasuring ground for the benefit and enjoyment of the people."

The spectacular scenery of Glacier National Park, which would be enjoyed by guests of the Great Northern Railway, was created by sheets of continental ice covering the land thousands of years ago:

> At least four major ice ages, separated in time by much longer interglacial periods, have spread enormous glaciers over wide areas of the northern continents during the last 3 million years ... The last ice age ended, and the present interglacial period began approximately 10,000 years ago.[7]

This continental glaciation process carved out huge U-shape valleys that were filled with water when the glaciers melted. This formed the largest lakes in the park—Lake McDonald on the west side and St. Mary Lake on the east side. The glaciers left behind jagged peaks of rock known as "horns," examples of which are seen at Logan Pass today with Mount Reynolds and Mount Clements. The Garden Wall in Glacier was created by immense sheets of ice on the east and west, leaving this rugged rock wall jutting up in their midst. The glaciers deposited massive piles of ground-up rocks known as moraines at their terminus and on their sides. The road into Many Glacier today is built upon an ancient glacial moraine that is constantly shifting and slumping, causing continual road damage.

The few glaciers that remain in the park today are not continental glaciers, but mountain glaciers formed over thousands of years by snowfall compacted into ice. Visitors to the park who hike to Grinnell Glacier or Sperry Glacier today can view the glaciers' terminal moraines and see the melting ice and deep crevasses of the glaciers. However, climate change is drastically reducing the size of these glaciers, and scientists predict the possibility that there will be no glaciers left in Glacier National Park in the 2030s. Hopefully, though, the spectacular scenery created by continental glaciation will remain to inspire visitors for generations to come.

Native Americans have utilized this glaciated landscape for thousands of years. Their descendants are the Flathead tribe on the west side of Glacier and the Blackfeet tribe on the east side of Glacier. The Flathead tribe ventured into Glacier to hunt mountain sheep and goats, deer, and elk. The Blackfeet tribe was content to hunt buffalo on the great plains to the east of Glacier. Neither tribe established settlements within the park, though temporary hunting camps were set up. Fighting between the tribes erupted when the Flathead crossed Glacier's passes and sought to hunt buffalo on Blackfeet territory. The Blackfeet fiercely defended their territory, just as they did when the first white men entered their land seeking beaver pelts. Their "attempts to penetrate into the country of the Blackfeet more often then [*sic.*] not resulted in a 'hair-raising' party, at which the Indians were more adept than the white man."[8]

The Lewis and Clark expedition reached the east side of Glacier in 1806. Meriwether Lewis had a camp at "'Camp Disappointment' between today's Cut Bank and Browning, Montana."[9] They encountered hostile Piegan Indians, killed two of them, and then escaped the area with their lives. "The Piegan and other Blackfoot tribes would remain hostile to almost any American presence in or near their territory," for nearly the next eighty years.[10]

Blackfeet tepees set up on the shore of Two Medicine Lake with Sinopah Mountain across the lake, c. 1914. (*Photograph by R. E. Marble, NPS GLAC6021*)

Smallpox, a deadly disease introduced by mountain men and traders, eventually caused the Blackfeet to lose their tenacious grip upon their territory. The Blackfeet had no defense against smallpox, and it decimated the tribe. Weak and dying, tribe members were unable to hunt for food, and starvation killed even more in 1883–84. Help eventually came from an unexpected source—a white man. James Willard Schultz was an easterner who loved New York's mountainous area. In 1877, at the age of eighteen, he left for the mountains of the northwest:

> He quickly took up with mountain men Hugh Monroe and Joe Kipp and became friends with Tail Feathers Coming-over-the Hill and other Piikani [Piegan]. He learned their language, lived as they lived, and joined them on hunts. The Piikani gave him the name Apikuni, meaning Spotted Robe, and at age twenty he married the Piikani woman Fine Shield. Schultz soon began writing about his adventures in the Rocky Mountains. His first stories were printed in the sports magazine *Forest and Stream.*[11]

The editor of *Forest and Stream* was George Bird Grinnell, an avid hunter and outdoorsman. Schultz wrote about the plight of the Blackfeet in a letter to Grinnell and urged him to visit the area. Grinnell visited the reservation in the spring of 1885 and was then successful in getting government aid to the Blackfeet increased.

> Grinnell was also introduced to the mountainous region of the reservation—particularly the area of St. Mary Lakes. With Schultz and Otokomi [Yellow Fish] as his guides, Grinnell explored and hunted in the region.[12]

Grinnell was enchanted with Glacier and returned for a second visit in 1887. This time, he explored the Many Glacier valley and climbed up to a large glacier that would soon bear his name: Grinnell Glacier. Grinnell wrote many articles about the wonders of Glacier in his magazine, and he, along with James J. Hill of the Great Northern Railway, became major proponents for the establishment of Glacier National Park.

Grinnell returned to Glacier again in October 1888 and tried to coax his companion, George Gould, to climb to Grinnell Glacier and not let the cold weather discourage him. Grinnell told his companion:

> What if we do freeze by day and dry up in the smoke by night? Have we not glorious appetites? Do we not sleep well? Does not our circulation recharge itself? Go to! We will become dirty and profane ... and we will enjoy life![13]

Future trips to Glacier for adventurers such as Grinnell were made much easier by the completion of the Great Northern Railway along Glacier's southern boundary in 1891. Riders could board the train at St. Paul, Minnesota, and arrive at Glacier two and a half days later. In 1894, the railway encouraged Dr. Lyman B. Sperry (a professor of geology and zoology at Oberlin College in Ohio) to ride the train to Glacier and "look for glaciers," which the railway could publicize in its promotional brochures. Sperry stayed with Charlie Howe in his cabin at Apgar on Lake McDonald. From there over the summers of 1894, 1895, and 1896, Sperry explored the area east of Lake McDonald, including the Avalanche Lake Basin, above which Sperry indeed found a glacier. This

Right: George and Elizabeth Grinnell on Grinnell Glacier during their final trip to Glacier in 1926. (*NPS*)

Below: This *c.* 1910 photograph by Fred Kiser shows the extent of Grinnell Glacier below the Garden Wall. In later years, the upper and lower portions of the glacier would become disconnected, with the upper portion becoming known as "Salamander" Glacier. Gem Glacier rests in the notch just to the right of Mount Gould, the tall peak at the left. Grinnell Lake, below, receives melt water from the glaciers. (*NPS GLAC7688*)

became known as Sperry Glacier, and Sperry "later was responsible for the building of the first trail to this glacier over approximately the same route as the present one."[14]

Thus, in the 1890s, conservationists, politicians, and railroad baron James J. Hill all took up the cry to preserve Glacier as a national park. Grinnell wrote an article for *Century Magazine* in which he called Glacier "The Crown of the Continent." Conservationist John Muir visited the Glacier area and called it "the best care-killing scenery on the continent." President Theodore Roosevelt set the precedent for Glacier National Park:

> [He preserved] five national parks, eighteen national monuments (courtesy of the Antiquities Act), four national game preserves, fifty-one bird sanctuaries, and 15 national forests—a total of 230 million acres in federal land.[15]

However, it remained for the Great Northern Railway to make the final push for Glacier to become a national park:

> Grinnell and other influential preservationists ... carried their cause to James J. Hill and other Great Northern officials, who in turn gave the Montana Congressional delegation the task of advocating the legislation for a park ... Hill's influence apparently made the park possible ... and Dr. Sperry wrote that 'it is equally true that the proposition did not take on signs of life in Washington till the Great Northern officials had told [Montana] Senator Carter to "Go To It!"[16]

The legislation to make Glacier a national park was introduced on December 11, 1907, and it took Congress another two and a half years to debate, amend, and finally approve the legislation, which President Taft signed on May 11, 1910.

The Great Northern Railway had a major role in establishing Glacier as a national park because it was in their business interests to do so. Thus, we begin our examination of transportation in Glacier National Park with the Great Northern Railway in the following chapter.

1

Trains to the Park

From the late 1800s to the early 1900s, every major western railroad played a role in promoting and preserving areas as national parks—for the Northern Pacific Railroad, it was Yellowstone and Mt. Rainier; for the Union Pacific, it was Yellowstone; for the Southern Pacific, it was Yosemite; for the Atchison, Topeka and Santa Fe, it was the Grand Canyon; and for the Great Northern Railway, it was Glacier National Park.

> The managers of these lines were motivated more by a desire to promote tourism and increase profits than by altruism or environmental concern. Nevertheless, preservationists like John Muir came to recognize the value of forming an alliance with a powerful corporate group committed to similar goals, if not from similar ideals.[1]

It was just such an alliance between conservationists John Muir, George Bird Grinnell, and Great Northern Railway President James J. Hill that succeeded in creating Glacier National Park. Muir had visited the Glacier area in the 1890s and wrote about it in his book *Our National Parks*:

> Get off the track at Belton Station, and in a few minutes you will find yourself in the midst of what you are sure to say is the best care-killing scenery on the continent ... Give a month at least to this precious reserve.[2]

Creating a national park was probably the last thing on the mind of James J. Hill when he envisioned creating his transcontinental railroad from St. Paul, Minnesota, to Seattle, Washington. Hill was a hard-nosed businessman and a fierce competitor. He was born on September 16, 1838, in a log cabin in Ontario, Canada, on his parents' farm. A childhood accident with an arrow blinded him in one eye. This never slowed him down, though, because "James J. Hill was like the locomotives he sent west: a one-eyed, self-propelled engine of unstoppable force."[3]

First, though, he had some growing up to do. In 1856, at the age of eighteen, Hill left home heading for the Atlantic seacoast with the dream of becoming a sea captain. He was unable to find a ship that would take him on, so he decided to head for the west seacoast. He got as far as St. Paul, Minnesota, where he missed the final wagon train heading west for the season. He secured a job in St. Paul as a shipping clerk for a Mississippi River steamboat company, and his lifelong career in transportation began. Hill's apprenticeship as a clerk introduced him to the cutthroat world of freight and shipping, and he quickly learned the trade. He tried to enlist for the Union in the Civil War but was not accepted for the army because of his blind eye.

During his time in St. Paul, Hill closely monitored the development of the new railroad technology. He became fascinated with railroads, and in 1866, he became a freight agent for the St. Paul and Pacific Railroad. He also became involved in the Northwestern Fuel Company which supplied coal to the railroad. His activities brought him a fair amount of wealth and in 1878 he purchased the St. Paul and Pacific. In 1879, the railroad became the St. Paul, Minneapolis and Manitoba Railway, as, backed by funds from Canadian investors, tracks were laid all the way to Winnipeg, the capital of Manitoba. Hill became the general manager of the railroad. By May 1879, the railroad had completed 565 miles of track across Minnesota and into Dakota Territory.

> It has been said of other sections of the American West that they were settled from the ox cart or covered wagon, while "Hill Country" was settled from the boxcar. Hill laid his rails first, and then labored tirelessly to create traffic for his trains. The success of his plans for rapid expansion depended upon quick and sound colonization.[4]

Hill recognized the great potential for farming in the Dakota Territory, and he became an expert on agriculture and livestock. His trains brought in thousands of European migrants, and he taught them how to grow wheat and what type of stock to raise. The trains would take the agricultural products raised in the Dakotas back to the growing eastern markets, and Hill kept his freight rates low so his farmers could ship out their products and make a profit. The trains also brought in needed manufactured supplies to the farmers, such as plows from the eastern industrial areas, again at reasonable prices, for the farmers to purchase. Except for a small area in Minnesota, Hill had no land grants from the federal government for his railroad, in contrast to all the other transcontinental railroads that were being built. He sold the land from the land grant:

> [He sold it] to the numerous and eager Norwegian and Swedish immigrants arriving in the United States, bringing in over $13 million for the railroad. Good harvest seasons for the next several years brought more business to his railroad ... Hill's campaign was successful. Forty thousand immigrants were plowing fields, planting crops, and building farms and towns on the Canadian and American sides of the Red River Valley by 1881.[5]

While Hill was anxious for his railroad to reach the west coast, he also realized that he had to continue financing the route himself, mile by mile, populating the land with revenue-producing farmers. It took until 1886 for the St. Paul, Minneapolis and Manitoba Railway to reach Minot in Dakota Territory. In 1887, the line was extended another 545 miles to Great Falls, Montana Territory. Hill accomplished this with the labor of 8,000 men and 3,300 draft horses.[6] He was relentless in pushing his laborers westward.

> He directed the construction, ramrodded the work, and drove his men through the blistering heat of summer and bitter cold of winter to lay one mile of track a day ... Hill walked the grade, watched the men, called them by their first names, and kept a frugal eye on materials. When snow piled high and slowed work, Hill got out of his private car and started shoveling, sending some of the frostbitten, weary men in to drink coffee and warm up while he shoveled. He was alternately brutal or considerate, but he kept men working.[7]

James J. Hill had always been a shrewd railroad man. Back in 1881, he purchased the Minneapolis & St. Cloud Railway, which had no trackage, but did have the Minnesota land grant that he needed. On September 18, 1889, Hill changed the name of the Minneapolis & St. Cloud Railway to the Great Northern Railway, with his eye clearly focused on reaching the Pacific Coast. Then on February 1, 1890, Hill's Great Northern took over the assets of the St. Paul, Minneapolis and Manitoba Railway. The new Great Northern Railway was poised to make its run to the coast. Construction began in April 1890 at Havre, Montana (Montana became a state on November 8, 1889). It was still 850 miles to Seattle, and the rugged Rocky Mountains had to be crossed to get there.

Hill was determined to find a low pass across the Rockies to avoid steep grades, curves, and the expenses those would incur. Since the Lewis and Clark expedition of 1806, rumors of the existence of a low pass had persisted. Lewis and Clark found a river that came out of the mountains and joined the Missouri River in Montana. Lewis named the river Maria's River for his cousin Maria Wood. It was reasoned that there must be a pass in the mountains where the river originated, and the river and the pass became known as the Marias River and Marias Pass, dropping the apostrophe from the name. Remarkably, it took until 1889 for a white man to discover the pass. This was largely due to the hostility of the Blackfeet Indians and their desire to keep the white people out. They closely guarded the secret of the location of Marias Pass. By 1885, though, the Blackfeet were decimated by smallpox and starvation, so they could not keep explorers from finding the pass.

This is one of the earliest logos of the Great Northern Railway, which was officially formed on February 1, 1890, when founder James J. Hill combined his Minneapolis and St. Cloud Railway with the St. Paul, Minneapolis and Manitoba Railway. The logo featured a depiction of the Rocky Mountain goat, which soon became a symbol of both the railway and Glacier National Park. (*Author's collection*)

Hill hired a very experienced mountain-country surveyor and engineer named John F. Stevens to find the pass for the Great Northern Railway. Grace Flandrau, writing in *The Story of Marias Pass,* a Great Northern booklet published in the late 1920s, paid tribute to the engineering skills of Stevens:

> Travelers, unless they happen to be civil engineers, which, of course, most of them are not, are in the habit of taking the passing of railroads through mountain ranges, entirely for granted. As the train advances, the apparently impenetrable mass which blocked the sky-line conveniently opens and arranges itself to accommodate an almost level road-bed.[8]

Pushed onward by Hill to find this "almost level road-bed," Stevens and his Flathead Indian guide set out to find the pass in December of 1889.

> [Stevens] followed the Marias River because of what he had heard in the Indian legends, but it was the middle of the winter in the Rockies and traveling was difficult. He kept hiking into the mountains—even after his Indian guide left him—and in his words "walked right into the pass." The snow was too deep for him to build a fire, so to keep from freezing to death he had to tramp back and forth until morning.[9]

Stevens survived his ordeal at the pass, and reported to Hill "that the pass was broad and open, the pass is a low open valley from 1 to 6 miles wide, the summit only 5,200 feet high and could be reached by a grade of less than 100 feet to the mile."[10]

By April 1890, construction of the Great Northern Railway proceeded west from Havre. One year later, in April 1891, workers started laying track west from Cut Bank, Montana, and by September, they had reached Marias Pass. Crossing the Continental Divide, the railroad followed Bear Creek to the Middle Fork of the Flathead River, which it then followed northwest, establishing a depot consisting of two boxcars at Belton, named for the construction crews' camp cook, Andrew Belton. From there, it proceeded to Kalispell, Montana, which was reached on December 31, 1891. Ahead lay the rugged Cascade Mountains of Washington, and it took the Great Northern another year to complete the route through the mountains to Seattle. James J. Hill drove the final spike on January 6, 1893.

The Great Northern Railway was the last railroad to complete its transcontinental route. The Union Pacific was completed in 1869; the Northern Pacific in 1883; the Southern Pacific also in 1883; and the Atchison, Topeka and Santa Fe in 1885. However, the Great Northern was the only transcontinental railroad to actually touch the boundary of a national park. When Glacier National Park was created in 1910, the Great Northern tracks followed the park's southern boundary for 60 miles. The Great Northern had passenger stops at the southeastern border of Glacier at Midvale (later named East Glacier) and at the southwestern border at Belton (the town was later named West Glacier). Thus, when Glacier became a national park, it already had rail service to its southern entry points.

Hill had accomplished his goal of reaching the West Coast. His railroad from St. Paul to Seattle stretched 1,816 miles, was 115 miles shorter than his rival Northern Pacific Railroad, and the Great Northern reached a national park. Hill, ever the astute

Right: The Great Northern Railway erected this statue in Marias Pass in 1925 to honor John F. Stevens, who had discovered the pass in 1889. (*Photograph by the author*)

Below: This 1930s map of the Great Northern Railway shows the route from Chicago to Glacier National Park and on west to Seattle. (*Author's collection*)

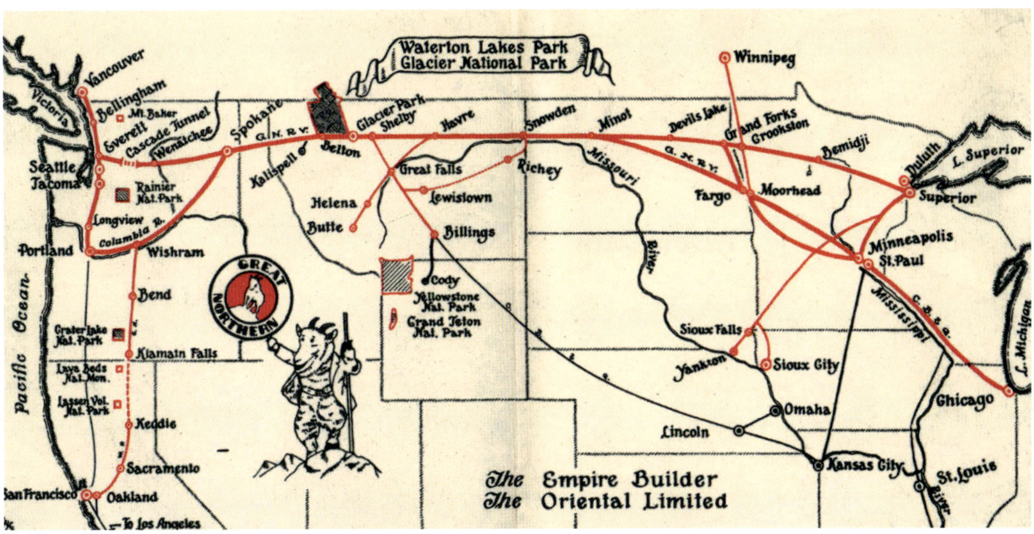

Glacier Park Station at Midvale on the park's southeastern corner, in the final stages of construction in early 1912. Note the cut logs on the right. (*From a photo in a historic display at the station*)

Glacier Park Station in the 1950s. Note the automobile on the drive and the Great Northern boxcar to the left. Passengers departing the train could walk between the station and Glacier Park Lodge along the path seen in the photo. Abundant flower displays lined the path all the way to the hotel. (*NPS GLAC11078a*)

businessman, recognized the potential of the Glacier area as a tourist destination, and in 1892, his railroad brought the first permanent settlers to Glacier. The families got off the train at Belton, headed north to Lake McDonald, which was 3 miles away, and built their first cabins.

> Charlie Howe, Milo Apgar, and Frank Gedhun, all built homes at the foot of the lake ... Milo Apgar and Charlie Howe began to cater to the visitors who occasionally got off the train at Belton and wanted to see Lake McDonald. Mrs. Apgar began to furnish meals.[11]

Other settlers constructed cabins at the head of Lake McDonald, including Denny Comeau, George Snyder, and Frank Kelly. In the late 1890s, Snyder built a hotel there to accommodate visitors from the train. When a bridge was built across the Middle Fork of the Flathead River in 1897, Snyder and Apgar formed a stage service to transport visitors between Belton and Lake McDonald. In 1898, Snyder began running a 40-foot steamboat on Lake McDonald, to transport tourists from Apgar's settlement to his hotel. Thus, a rudimentary transportation system was created by road from Belton to Lake McDonald (Apgar) and by boat from Apgar to Snyder's hotel. All this activity had been made possible by the Great Northern transporting settlers to their departure point at Belton.

In 1892, the Great Northern began developing facilities in Marias Pass to service its locomotives. A water tower was constructed, and a railyard was developed with a 60-foot turntable. This development took on the name of "Summit," and subsequent construction there included a tool house, section house, and agent house. A depot was built in 1906 and it was replaced in 1928 by a larger structure, built in what had become, by then, the Great Northern traditional alpine style.

Approximately 16 miles west of Summit, the Great Northern built a rail facility at Essex. Its purpose was to station helper locomotives there to get trains up the steep eastbound grade to Marias Pass. At Marias Pass, the helper locomotives would be cut off, turned on the turntable, and returned to Essex. Great Northern facilities at Essex included three water towers, a coal tower, a turntable, a depot, and a section house.

> The yard was named Essex. probably for one of the railroaders, and then changed to "Walton" in 1926 when many Great Northern Railway stations were renamed to promote Glacier country's historical lore. Walton was named for the famous bait and fly fisherman Izaak Walton, who wrote *The Compleat* [*sic.*] *Angler* in 1653, a book still considered the fisherman's bible. Later, the town would take back its original name of Essex and the Izaak Walton Inn would continue to be a tribute to the old fisherman.[12]

So today, the Izaak Walton Inn is located in Essex on the west side of the Middle Fork of the Flathead River, and the National Park Service ranger station on the east side of the river is named Walton.

Heavy snowfall from Walton to East Glacier required the Great Northern to hire crews to remove the snow from the tracks for nine months of the year. The crews were housed at Essex in appalling conditions, such as tents and abandoned boxcars. It became difficult for the railroad to find snow-shoveling crews willing to live in such conditions, so in April 1939, the Great Northern contracted to build a hotel at Essex.

The Great Northern Railway constructed the Belton Chalet in 1910 to serve guests departing for Glacier National Park. At mid-left in the photo is Belton Station, a significant improvement over the two boxcars that originally served as a depot. (*Fred Kiser photograph, 1911, NPS GLAC7671*)

This westward view by Fred Kiser in 1911 clearly shows the relationship between the Belton Station and the chalet, with a wagon road leading up from the station to the chalet. The effects of the forest fire of 1910 are seen beyond the boxcars on the right. (*Oregon Historical Society Library, ba021214*)

Belton Station still serves passengers today as eastbound and westbound Amtrak trains stop here. On August 15, 1991, Amtrak awaits passengers for its early morning departure eastbound from Belton. (*Photograph by the author*)

Summit Station at Marias Pass built in the Great Northern's traditional alpine style, photographed by George Grant on August 5, 1932. (*NPS GLACGrant9*)

The hotel was completed in November 1939 and was built rather luxuriously to house both railroad crews and tourists. It had twenty-nine rooms and ten bathrooms, with a dining room, and a recreation room in the basement. It was envisioned that the hotel would serve as a midway entrance to Glacier National Park, between East Glacier and West Glacier. However, the advent of World War II killed these plans. Today, though, the quaint Izaak Walton Hotel serves visitors year-round with hikers in the summer and cross-country skiers in the winter. There is a bridge from the hotel over the train tracks to the hill on the other side, where the hotel has parked several railroad caboose cars and transformed them into cottages for visitors.

In 1907, at the age of sixty-nine, James J. Hill finally stepped down as president of the Great Northern Railway and became chairman of the board. When he retired as chairman of the board in 1912, the great "Empire Builder," as he was widely known, proudly stated: "Most men who have really lived have had in some shape, their great adventure. This railway is mine."[13]

His son, Louis W. Hill, age thirty-five, then became president of the railway. Louis was much more interested in advertising and building hotels than he was in running a railroad, so he turned those duties over to his assistant Ralph Budd. "Louis was intelligent enough to realize he could not replace [his father]. 'There was not room in one family for more than one 'Empire Builder,' he said."[14]

In 1912, Louis stepped down as president of the Great Northern and became chairman of the board. In this role, he could really let his creative advertising juices flow. Louis realized that in the early 1900s, America was losing wealthy tourists to Europe. Tourists would not come to western national parks unless there were luxurious accommodations for them. Beginning in 1910, Louis began a building spree in and around Glacier National Park that would provide such accommodations for the wealthy. Glacier would become the "Switzerland of America" and travelers would be encouraged to "See America First." These slogans soon appeared in Great Northern advertising brochures.

The first lodging Louis Hill constructed was the Belton Chalet, built in 1910 in the Swiss-chalet style of architecture. The chalet was directly south of the train station and was connected to it by a trellised walkway and a wagon path. However, Louis wanted to establish Great Northern headquarters on the east side of Glacier. The railroad station at Midvale (East Glacier) was nearing completion in 1912, yet it was on the Blackfeet Reservation. Hill realized that he could not build his headquarters hotel on the reservation, so in 1912, he purchased 160 acres of the reservation from the Blackfeet, just west of the station. Construction of the signature Glacier Park Lodge then began, and it was completed in time for the summer season of 1913 at a cost of $500,000.

Seven more lodgings, all in the chalet style, were completed by 1915—St. Mary Chalet on St. Mary Lake; Going-to-the-Sun Chalet at Sun Point; Two Medicine Chalet on Two Medicine Lake; Cut Bank Chalet; Gunsight Lake Chalet; Sperry Chalet on the trail to Sperry Glacier; Granite Park Chalet on the west side of the Garden Wall; and Many Glacier Chalets on the hillside above Lake McDermott (later renamed Swiftcurrent Lake). Unfortunately, Gunsight Lake Chalet was destroyed by an avalanche in the winter of 1916 and never rebuilt.

With the exception of St. Mary and Cut Bank, the chalets could only be reached on horseback or by boat, so they offered a chance for the more adventurous visitors to see the interior of Glacier National Park and stay in relatively comfortable accommodations.

The Izaak Walton Hotel was completed in 1939 at Essex to house Great Northern railroad crews clearing the line of snow. It was also designed to serve tourists entering the midpoint of Glacier's southern boundary. (*Photograph by the author, July 25, 2012*)

An Amtrak passenger train cruises past the Izaak Walton Hotel on July 25, 2012. Due to increasing summer and winter tourist traffic, this is now a regular stop on the Amtrak line. (*Photograph by the author*)

Above: The path mid-left leads to the pedestrian bridge over the railroad tracks. It connects the Izaak Walton Hotel with caboose lodges on the hill on the other side. (*Photograph by the author, July 25, 2012*)

Below left: The Izaak Walton Hotel has parked several cabooses on the hill opposite the hotel. Cabooses have been converted to comfortable lodging for guests. (*Photograph by the author, July 25, 2012*)

Below right: The cover of a Great Northern Railway advertising pamphlet from the 1920s; this featured the railway's mountain goat logo along with the slogan "See America First." (*Author's collection*)

This photograph from 1914 shows Glacier Park Lodge, which was completed in 1913. The grand log archway stood between the railroad station and the hotel. Blackfeet Indians, paid by the Great Northern Railway, set up tepees on the lawn. Later, a large annex was built on the left side of the hotel, nearly doubling its size. (*NPS*)

For the really daring visitor, tent camps were set up even farther in the interior of the park, and horses could be ridden from the chalets to the tent camps. The tents were wall-type tents with wooden floors and beds with mattresses, so the visitor was still comfortable.

Louis Hill outdid himself with the completion of the Many Glacier Hotel, which was opened on the shore of Lake McDermott on July 4, 1915. This grand lodge was even larger than the Glacier Park Lodge at East Glacier. Also, Hill had even one more hotel up his sleeve—the Prince of Wales Hotel in Waterton Lakes National Park, Glacier's next-door neighbor across the border in Canada. Hill had proposed this hotel in 1913, but it was delayed by World War I. Construction finally began in 1926, and the hotel opened in July 1927.

With the construction of all these hotels, chalets, and tent camps, Hill needed to create a transportation network to connect them. He immediately began road-building efforts on the east side of Glacier to connect Glacier Park Lodge with St. Mary and then Many Glacier to the north.

> In 1912, Hill brought in Banff outfitters William and James Brewster to set up a saddle horse and stagecoach concession to operate between tent camps. On lakes and rivers where tour boats were needed, Hill contracted with Captain William Swanson to build the boats and run them for the railway ... In 1914, Hill arranged with Walter White of the White Motor Company to provide autobus services in the park and formed the Glacier Park Transportation Company to operate the little red buses.[15]

With the construction of all this infrastructure in Glacier, the Great Northern Railway had to be sure to also provide the best, most up-to-date passenger service on its trains.

Above left: The Many Glacier Hotel, Louis Hill's largest, was completed on the shore of Lake McDermott in 1915. It was surrounded by mountains offering hiking trails in every direction. (*Photograph by T. J. Hileman, c. 1926, NPS*)

Above right: The glorious Prince of Wales Hotel was completed by Louis Hill and the Great Northern Railway in July 1927, in Waterton Lakes National Park, Canada. The protective coverings over the large picture windows have not yet been removed for the summer season in this early June 1972 photograph taken by the author as part of a group of tour bus drivers participating in their orientation tour.

On June 18, 1893, James J. Hill launched the first Great Northern transcontinental passenger train service from St. Paul to Seattle, a seventy-two-hour run. The train was called the "Oriental Limited" to advertise Great Northern connections to Asia via their steamship lines from Seattle. A Chicago connection was added to the Oriental Limited's run in 1909 after Hill's stock buy-out of the Chicago, Burlington and Quincy Railroad. On June 10, 1929, the passenger train was renamed the "Empire Builder." The Great Northern advertised the Empire Builder as follows:

> A new all steel train that marks another forward step in the fulfillment of the plans of the railroad's founder, James J. Hill, and it is to honor him that the new train has taken the title Mr. Hill so richly merited—the Empire Builder.[16]

The departure of the Empire Builder from Chicago and St. Paul was timed such that the train crossed North Dakota in the dark and passed along Glacier National Park in the daylight, allowing passengers to enjoy the spectacular scenery. The Empire Builder trains were hauled by powerful Baldwin steam locomotives.

> Baldwin Locomotive Works, without question, was the favorite builder of the Great Northern and the road turned to Baldwin time after time both for new types of locomotives, and re-orders.[17]

Passenger train traffic came to a halt during World War II as the transcontinental trains were used to transport soldiers and equipment. Glacier closed its hotels during the war years and reopened them in 1946. The years after the war inaugurated the "streamliner" era, as the steam locomotives were replaced by diesels and the passenger cars were continually updated. Great Northern painted its diesels in an "Omaha Orange" and "Pullman Green" color scheme. Orange was the predominant color of the engines with green stripe trim. The same color scheme continued across all the passenger cars, producing a sleek streamliner look. The Empire Builder offered streamlined service from Chicago to Seattle in forty-five hours.

In 1955, the Great Northern purchased twelve "Vista Dome" coaches to add to streamliner service:

> The cars contained 46 leg rest seats and 24 dome seats for a total seating capacity of 70 passengers ... Among the most beautiful lounge cars ever built were the six Empire Builder [Great Dome] lounge cars in the "View" series, constructed by the Budd Company in 1955.[18]

The Great Dome cars were named the Glacier View, Ocean View, Mountain View, Lake View, Prairie View, and River View. On the Great Domes, the dome portion ran the full length of the car, and there were fifty-seven seats in the dome section with thirty-four seats in the lounge section on the lower level. Just imagine riding in the Glacier View dome along Glacier National Park's southern boundary—what a spectacular journey that would have been.

In 1967, the paint scheme of the Empire Builder was changed from Omaha Orange and Pullman Green to Big Sky Blue—an homage to Montana whose state slogan was "Big Sky Country," which harkened back to A. B. Guthrie's 1947 novel *The Big Sky.* The locomotives and the passenger cars were primarily a bright blue with a white stripe in the middle. In 1970, the paint scheme changed again with the merger of the Great Northern Railway with the Northern Pacific Railway (Hill's old archrival). The new railroad became the Burlington Northern, and it adopted a Cascade Green paint scheme with a predominant dark green color and a white stripe. One more color change came in 1995 when the Burlington Northern merged with the Santa Fe Pacific to form the Burlington Northern Santa Fe Railroad (BNSF). The BNSF brought back the old Omaha Orange and Pullman Green paint scheme for its diesel engines. However, this paint scheme would not be applied to passenger cars again because when Amtrak took over all passenger rail service on May 1, 1971, it gradually converted all passenger cars to silver trimmed in red, white, and blue.

> [In 1979] the Amtrak Empire Builder became the first long-distance train in the Amtrak fleet to receive the [double-decked] Superliners, which had an upper-level observation

The westbound Empire Builder pulls into Glacier Park Station on June 10, 1934, in this George Grant photograph. The steam locomotive was built by the Baldwin Locomotive Works in 1923 and had a 4-8-2 wheel alignment. (*NPS GLAC11498*)

Passengers depart from the Empire Builder at Glacier Park Station on June 10, 1934. They could walk approximately two blocks from the other side of the station to the Glacier Park Lodge. Bellhops were available to bring their luggage over to the hotel. (*Photograph by George Grant, NPS Grant0925*)

Amtrak's westbound Empire Builder pulls into Glacier Park Station on August 14, 2001, in this scene reminiscent of George Grant's 1934 photograph. (*Photograph by the author*)

The streamlined Empire Builder is eastbound in the early 1950s. The train has crossed Marias Pass and is reaching the Montana plains with Glacier National Park's mountains rising in the background. (*Great Northern Railway photograph*)

A wider view of the 1950s eastbound Empire Builder as it nears East Glacier. The streamliner is decked out in the paint scheme of "Omaha Orange" (the lighter color on the train) and "Pullman Green" (the darker color along the top and bottom of the train). (*Great Northern Railway photograph*)

The Empire Builder has left Belton and is heading east to tunnel number 4 along the Middle Fork of the Flathead River. Three "Vista Dome" cars can be seen at the end of the train, part of a group of twelve purchased by the Great Northern in 1955. The full-length "Great Dome" cars were added later in 1955. (*NPS GLAC_11097*)

> deck similar to the old Budd Great Dome cars that began service with the Empire Builder a quarter-century before.[19]

When Amtrak operates on time today, it takes the Empire Builder approximately forty-four hours and ten minutes to make the run from Chicago to Seattle. Glacier National Park is still traversed in the daylight hours.

We cannot leave the Great Northern Railway without discussing Louis Hill's brilliant advertising campaigns beginning in 1910. Besides his slogans of "See America First" and "Switzerland of America," he adopted the Rocky Mountain goat as the logo of the Great Northern. The "Great Northern was so identified with Glacier that the Great Northern goat became the symbol of both the railroad and Glacier National Park."[20] Over time, the goat became so familiar that he gained the nickname of "Rocky," and he appeared in all the Great Northern brochures and Glacier National Park advertising. Hill churned out promotional brochure after brochure with the goat and his slogans. In 1927, Louis Hill struck another advertising bonanza when he hired the artist Winold Reiss to paint portraits of the Blackfeet Indians. The colorful portraits were used on Great Northern calendars, brochures, and dining car menus for over thirty years.

The Great Northern always treated the Blackfeet with the utmost respect because "Blackfeet people were seen by the Great Northern as an essential part of the ethos of the Mountain West where the railroad took vacationers."[21] For their part, the Blackfeet

Above left: Five Burlington Northern Santa Fe locomotives head east across Marias Pass in July 2012. Four of the five locomotives are painted in the old Great Northern paint scheme of Omaha Orange and Pullman Green. (*Photograph by the author*)

Above right: Two Amtrak diesel locomotives pull the eastbound Empire Builder across Marias Pass on August 15, 1991. The Amtrak paint scheme of silver with red, white, and blue stripes is clearly visible. (*Photograph by the author*)

The eastbound Amtrak Empire Builder is crossing the trestle over Midvale Creek just before entering East Glacier and Glacier Park Station on August 15, 1991. (*Photograph by the author*)

The eastbound Amtrak Empire Builder has just left East Glacier's Glacier Park Station and is crossing the spectacular trestle over Two Medicine River on August 2, 1994. The train is completely equipped with the double-decked "Superliner" passenger cars. Glacier National Park's mountains rise in the background. (*Photograph by the author*)

A display of Winold Reiss Blackfeet painting reproductions at Glacier Park Station on July 25, 2012. Reiss' paintings were used in Great Northern calendars, brochures, menu covers, and playing cards. (*Photograph by the author*)

were glad to cooperate with the railroad because it brought them economic prosperity. They were paid for their portraits, photographs, and appearances in advertising and motion pictures. The Great Northern paid them to pose in traditional costume, meeting visitors at Glacier Park Station, and setting up tepees on the lawn of Glacier Park Lodge and other locations in the park.

Thus, Louis Hill's promotional campaigns paid off with the filling of his passenger train cars and his lodgings in and around Glacier National Park.

> To this day, the identities of the Empire Builder and Glacier National Park are inextricably linked. The Great Northern literally put the park on the map and helped define its image and relationship with its visitors in a way that is still seen to this day. No mention of the history of the railroad or the park is complete without mention of the other.[22]

Historical Spotlight: Artist Winold Reiss

Winold Reiss was born in Karlsruhe, Germany in 1888. The first thing to clear up is how to pronounce his name. In his excellent biography of Reiss, Scott Tanner states that "Just a few have figured out how to pronounce his uncommon name. The name is 'VEE-nold' Rice."[23] Growing up in Germany, Reiss was influenced by his father, who was a painter, and by reading James Fennimore Cooper's *Leatherstocking Tales*, which led to his lifelong interest in American Indians. Reiss received his art training at the Royal Academy of Fine Arts and the School of Applied Arts in Munich.

In 1912, he married Henriette Luthy, whom he had met at the school. With war looming in Europe, Reiss convinced his bride that they should emigrate to the United States, which they did in 1913. They landed in New York City, and Reiss immediately began painting, placing his work in galleries and restaurants in the city. In 1916, he opened an art school.

By 1919, Reiss had earned enough money to visit the American West and fulfill his dream of seeing "real" Indians. He got on the Great Northern Railway and traveled to Browning, Montana, on the Blackfeet Indian Reservation, just east of Glacier National Park. After some initial awkwardness in establishing relationships with the Blackfeet, he gained their trust and started painting their portraits in one of the rooms in the Haggerty Hotel in Browning. The Blackfeet were so astonished at his ability to produce lifelike portraits of them that they soon bonded with Reiss. Paul Raczka, owner of a trading post in Fort McLeod, said of the Blackfeet that "Winold, over time, earned their trust. He was, they knew, one white man who wasn't about to rip them off."[24] Within a month, Reiss had produced thirty-five portraits of the Blackfeet. Back in New York, Reiss sold the entire lot to Dr. Philip Cole, an important western art collector.

For the next eight years, Reiss continued teaching at his art school in New York. He convinced his brother, Hans, to leave Sweden in 1923 and join him in New York to

In the fall of 1919, Winold Reiss got off the Great Northern train in Browning, Montana, and started painting portraits of the Blackfeet Indians. He produced thirty-five portraits within a month. Beginning in 1927, Reiss' portraits appeared on Great Northern calendars for the next thirty years. (*Author's collection*)

teach at the art school; Hans specialized in sculpture. Hans suffered from hay fever, and New York City's climate was bad for him, so Winold suggested that Hans go to Glacier National Park in 1925. Hans went to the park and loved it, deciding to stay there. He became a licensed climbing guide in the park. As fate would have it, one of his climbing clients was Louis Hill of the Great Northern Railway. Hans mentioned his brother's painting skills and eventually sent photographs of some of Winold's Blackfeet portraits to Hill. Hill was instantly impressed and stated, "I think this man is one of the best prospects we have had in the way of artists painting Indian pictures, which are our strongest feature, and it takes a good artist to make them."[25] A contract was signed, and for ten years beginning in 1927, Reiss returned to Browning and Glacier every summer to paint for the Great Northern Railway. His images were used on Great Northern calendars for the next thirty years. Railway vice-president William Kenney stated, "So far as the Indian calendars are concerned, no one can do them justice as can Winold Reiss."[26]

Also in 1927, Louis Hill was opening the Prince of Wales Hotel in Waterton Lakes National Park in Canada, and he asked Reiss to travel to Canada to paint portraits of the local Blood Indians, who were relatives of the Blackfeet. These portraits were used to advertise the new hotel.

In 1934, Reiss suggested to Louis Hill the idea of establishing a summer art school in Glacier. Hill liked the idea and provided the St. Mary Chalets as the location. The chalets had been shuttered during the Great Depression, and Reiss' school would bring paying guests to the railroad and to the chalets. Hans Reiss assisted in the art school, teaching sculpture. The schools ran from 1934 to 1937, when they were discontinued. In 1935, to celebrate the twenty-fifth anniversary of the establishment of Glacier National Park, the Great Northern Railway published a book titled *Blackfeet Indians*, which featured forty-nine of Reiss' finest portraits. The book quickly became a collector's item and was long out of print before Gramercy Books republished it in 1995. After the summer art school closed in 1937, Reiss returned to New York, teaching in his school there, and occasionally returning to Glacier to paint in the summers.

In 1943, Hill and Reiss signed a new contract:

> For additional Blackfeet portraits for Great Northern calendars. That summer Reis completed sixty-six new portraits. Reiss' last trip to Glacier National Park was in 1948. [Reiss died in 1953 and] in July 1954 the Blackfeet tribe held a ceremony at Red Blanket Hill to honor him. George Bullchild led the group of mourners in traditional Blackfeet prayers and songs, then they scattered Reiss' ashes to the wind.[27]

Helen Appleton Read, writing in the 1935 book *Blackfeet Indians*, noted a certain irony about Winold Reiss:

> It is perhaps [a] paradox that a painter of German birth should have been a pathfinder in discovering the decorative possibilities of the North American Indian ... His pictures have helped to restore and give reality to the legend of the noble redman.[28]

Perhaps it is not ironic though, that an immigrant from Germany would have such a profound impact upon the Great Northern Railway, since its founder James J. Hill, was himself an immigrant from Canada.

2

Buses to the Hotels

When planning began for the construction of Louis Hill's two great hotels on the east side of Glacier National Park—Glacier Park Lodge at Midvale and the Many Glacier Hotel to the north—Louis Hill realized he had a problem on his hands: there was no direct road connecting the two hotels. Glacier National Park, headquartered at West Glacier, did not have money to build roads on the east side of the park. So, Hill put his railroad construction crews to the task. "The railroad's engineering and construction crews excelled in grading, alignment, bridge work, surveying, slope deviation, and drainage issues."[1]

Steam shovels and road graders set out north from Glacier Park Lodge to carve the road up to the Hudson Bay Divide and down to St. Mary Lake. From there, it was on north to Babb and then construction of the road west to Many Glacier, which was completed in 1913. Initially, horse-drawn carriages took passengers on the road. Within a year, though, the first automobiles appeared on the road, and horse teams became unmanageable when frightened by the noise of the new iron creatures.

In December 1913, Walter White of the White Motor Company approached Louis Hill about using the company's vehicles in Glacier. The White Motor Company was founded in Cleveland, Ohio, by Walter's father, Thomas White, in 1900. The company eventually produced autos, trucks, buses, and tractors, along with such products as sewing machines, bicycles, automatic lathes, and even roller skates. By 1913, White vehicles were being used for bus service in 300 communities and in Rainier National Park in Washington.

> Hill agreed to let White test his buses (in Glacier) during the 1914 season. On June 13, 1914, $40,000 worth of vehicles were unloaded at Glacier Park Station. The vehicles included ten 11-passenger buses, five 7-passenger touring cars and two 2-ton trucks.[2]

The equipment had to be parked under trees at East Glacier because there was no garage. With the subsequent acceptance of the vehicles from White, the Great Northern Railway built a garage at East Glacier late in 1914. However, Louis Hill had no desire to run a bus company.

> The Great Northern formed a partnership in 1914 with the Glacier Park Transportation Company, run by Roe Emery. The company replaced the previous horse and stage operation and introduced gleaming new tour buses produced by the White Motor Company.[3]

The original buses were open-style and did not have canvas tops or windows as did the later models. The tops were wood, supported by iron braces with linen side curtains between the braces. The curtains could be rolled up to allow the passengers views of the park, or they could be rolled down to keep out wind, dust, and rain. The new roads were in terrible condition though, especially with the heavy rains in the summer of 1915. A female passenger recalled, "There were never enough spare tires or willing hands capable of pushing the bus out of the swollen ruts."[4] Enterprising teamsters stood by with their horses at notoriously muddy bogs and pulled the stuck buses out.

Bus drivers were scarce in 1915, as the populace was just learning to drive automobiles and buses.

> Roe Emery realized the unique role his drivers played as park tour guides and was proud and protective of them. Drivers were paid at rates substantially higher than most other park employees, at one time earning $100 a month compared to $30 paid to bellhops ... At East Glacier drivers had separate housing.[5]

The terrible roads soon took a toll on the condition of the buses. By the mid-1920s, they were wearing out. A series of new buses was ordered from the White Motor Company between 1925 and 1927. These buses had a fold-back top and a baggage compartment welded onto the frame at the rear. "At its height under Roe Emery, the fleet numbered sixty-six, with as many as seventy drivers hired each season to meet schedules."[6]

The opening of the Going-to-the-Sun Road across the Continental Divide in the heart of Glacier in 1933 caused more problems for the bus fleet. The buses simply were not up to the demand of the rigorous journey from Lake McDonald up and over Logan Pass, and down to the east side of the park. The Glacier Park Transport Company took their concerns to the White Motor Company; a stronger bus was needed to climb over the mountains. White responded with their Model 706 chassis. In 1935, a four-way competition was held by the National Park Service at Yosemite National Park to determine which company's bus would best serve the need of western mountain parks. Ford, GMC, REO, and the White Motor Company were the competitors. The White Motor Company Model 706 won the competition to carry passengers through eight western national parks—Glacier, Yellowstone, Grand Canyon, Mt. Rainier, Rocky Mountain, Yosemite, Bryce, and Zion.

White manufactured 500 of these buses, and thirty-five were delivered to Glacier National Park between 1936 and 1939—nineteen buses arrived in 1936, followed by eleven in 1937, four in 1938, then one in 1939. The Transport Company numbered the buses in order from the arrival of the very first buses, so that Bus Number 88 was the eighty-eighth bus ordered from White, and so on. These are the numbers that are still seen on the side of the buses today.

This 1930s recreational map of Glacier appeared in a Great Northern Railway promotional brochure. In the lower left corner, the Empire Builder train brings passengers to Glacier Park Hotel at East Glacier. From there, the Great Northern's transportation system within the park took over, with open-top tour buses taking tourists to the other Great Northern hotels—

Lake McDonald Hotel, Many Glacier Hotel, and the Prince of Wales Hotel. From the hotels, horses took visitors to the back-country chalets. Also, boats cruised the lakes, carrying passengers to hiking trails. (*Author's collection*)

In 1914, the first generation of White buses picked up passengers from the Glacier Park Station (roof eave seen at extreme mid-left). The two buses were followed by a horse-drawn carriage. In 1915, horse-drawn transportation was eliminated on park roads. (*Photograph by R. E. Marble, NPS GLAC6147*)

A tour bus is parked at St. Mary Chalet, *c.* 1914. The first generation of White tour buses had a wood top supported by iron bars attached to the sides of the frame. The bus was open-air with canvas drapes, which could be lowered from the top to keep out wind, dust, and rain. The chalet was on the south side of St. Mary Lake, with Singleshot Mountain seen across the lake, and a tour boat docked, waiting for passengers. (*Library of Congress, LC-USZ62-100931*)

Thirteen female passengers posed with a second-generation White tour bus at the Hudson's Bay Divide in 1926 on the road from East Glacier to St. Mary. These buses had a roll back top and a baggage compartment at the rear. Jammer Ector Bossati took the photo of the women and wrote on the back of the photo, "one of my bus loads!" (*NPS GLAC HPF4067*)

In 1932, three second-generation tour buses make their way slowly down the Blackfeet Highway (as the road between East Glacier and St. Mary was known). St. Mary Lake is seen in the valley below. (*Photograph by T. J. Hileman, NPS GLAC10188*)

These are supposedly the first buses crossing the newly opened Going-to-the-Sun Road over Logan Pass on July 15, 1933. The first bus was driven by Aubrey Chapman and the second bus by Bill Lindsay. (*Photograph by T. J. Hileman, NPS GLAC HPF2232*)

After the Going-to-the-Sun Road was opened over Logan Pass in 1933, the second-generation White buses soon proved unable to take the strain of the steep, winding road. By 1935, new buses were needed, and the first of the third-generation White buses (shown here) were delivered to Glacier in 1936. These are the buses which still operate in Glacier Park today. The scene, *c.* 1950, is at the Wild Goose Island overlook on St. Mary Lake. (*Photograph by Walt Dyke for the Great Northern Railway, NPS GLAC_109366*)

The new buses for Glacier were painted a bright red, reflecting the color of the Mountain Ash berry commonly seen in the park. The buses, still in use today, are 25 feet long, have five doors on the passenger side in addition to the driver's door on the left side, have a retractable canvas roof, and can carry seventeen passengers.

> The Red Buses are ... ornate. Conceived during a time when art deco was a cultural movement, the buses project the elegance, glamour, and strength of an era that valued the perceived modern image ... The Red Buses are mobile art.[7]

While the buses are "mobile art," there is also an art to driving them. Originally, drivers had to double-clutch to change gears. This often resulted in a loud grinding noise as the driver fought to find the right gear. Thus, drivers earned the nickname "gear jammers," or "jammers" for short.

Glacier's drivers are still fondly known as jammers today, although the manual bus transmissions have long since been replaced by automatic transmissions. A common joke in the 1970s when this author was driving red bus number 97 was to tell new drivers that they had to double-clutch the buses. So on their first drive over the mountain from East Glacier to Two Medicine, the newbie was furiously trying to double-clutch and the trainer was laughing hilariously, finally telling the jammer that the transmissions were no longer double-clutch; a single-clutch would suffice.

In 1936, the Transport Company developed the Driver's Manual to be sure jammers were giving tourists accurate information about Glacier Park. The manual was a 200-page book "chock full of practical information." It was edited by Glacier's Chief Park Naturalist George Ruhle. It was updated several times over the years. The red buses were operated in 1942, then shut down during World War II for the summers of 1943, 1944, and 1945. Tours resumed in the summer of 1946.

In December 1960, Don Hummel, a former mayor of Tucson, Arizona, bought the hotels and bus company from the Great Northern Railway and formed Glacier Park Inc. "To keep the Whites operating, Hummel had their original straight-six motors replaced with International Harvester and GM engines."[8] Remarkably, the buses kept running until 1999, racking up an incredible average of 600,000 miles each since their acquisition in the 1930s.

In July 1999, "a red bus had just dropped off a load of passengers at Lake McDonald Lodge. As the bus was driving away at low speed, its front axle parted from the frame."[9] Further examination revealed stress fractures in the chassis of three buses, and all buses were pulled out of service. They were replaced with thirty white Dodge 15-passenger vans at a cost of about $800,000. There was speculation that the red buses would never return to Glacier. "Both the Park Service and the concessioner were inclined to retire them permanently and purchase a new fleet. Their initial impression was that the buses might be too decrepit to restore."[10] However, public outcry was virtually unanimous—save the historic Glacier Park buses. Thankfully, the Ford Motor Company came to the rescue.

A plan was developed to have Glacier Park Inc. donate the buses to the National Park Foundation, a non-profit organization. Thus, Ford's contribution of $6.5 million to the Foundation for the restoration of the buses was tax-deductible. The restoration was a very challenging process. Bruce Gordon, director of Ford's alternative fuel vehicles, said:

Above left: Jammers studying the 1940 Driver's Manual at the East Glacier jammer dorm. The manual was edited by George Ruhle, Glacier's chief park naturalist. (*Photograph from a display at Glacier Park Station*)

Above right: Glacier Park Lodge in East Glacier, *c.* 1950. The jammer dorm was about four blocks down the road to the right. Flower beds lined the walkways from the train station (just off the bottom of the photo) to the hotel. The bus could take passengers and luggage to the hotel if they did not want to walk from the station. (*Photograph by Fred Noble for the Great Northern Railway, NPS GLAC_1109a*)

"Restoring the Red Buses has been a bigger challenge than any of us imagined, but it has also been a labor of love to those involved. We worked diligently to maintain the historic integrity of the buses."[11]

The first of the restored buses returned to Glacier in June 2002, and Jim Maddy, president of the National Park Foundation, summed up the importance of the occasion: "There is no more representative symbol of Glacier National Park than these classic Red Buses."[12]

In 2018, the buses were rehabilitated again, under the terms of the concession contract awarded to Xanterra in 2014. The engines were replaced with an electric hybrid system in order to reduce fuel consumption and emissions. Hopefully, this will enable the red buses to keep rolling for a long time into the future.

Since the red buses provided the only means of transportation other than saddle horses, between the Great Northern Railway hotels in Glacier during the early years, it is appropriate to delve briefly into the history of each. The first hotel constructed by Louis Hill was Glacier Park Lodge in East Glacier.

> Louis Hill had a definite vision of what he wanted for his entrance hotel. It had to be big, massive to the point of surpassing every natural and man-made object in the

> vicinity. The eastern entrance of Glacier Park had to tweak visitors' imaginations and desire to explore and see the wonders beyond.[13]

Construction of the hotel began in March 1912 and it was opened on June 15, 1913. It initially consisted of a lobby, dining room, and sixty-one guest rooms. A railroad spur was built from Glacier Park Station to the hotel construction site in order to bring in the massive log pillars for the hotel. The timbers were hauled in by rail flat car from Washington and Oregon, and each weighed approximately 15 tons, measured 36 to 42 inches in diameter, and were over 50 feet in length.

> [The hotel] lobby [is] 200 feet in length and 100 feet in width. Outlining the center of the lobby stand 30 pillars, each a massive Douglas fir column with its bark still intact ... The log pillars rise 52 feet from the basement to the ceiling.[14]

It soon became apparent that the hotel did not have enough rooms for all the passengers arriving on the Great Northern Railway. Louis Hill then ordered construction of an annex south of the hotel, consisting of an additional 111 rooms. It was completed within the next year. Hill could then concentrate on road building, so White buses could motor on north to his next hotel at Many Glacier.

Louis Hill conceived the Many Glacier Hotel when he visited the site at Lake McDermott (now Swiftcurrent Lake) in 1909, before Glacier even became a national park. He established a tepee camp there in 1912 with ten tents to accommodate forty people arriving on horseback. In 1913, he had eight log cabins (the Many Glacier Chalets) built on the slope of Mount Altyn overlooking the lake. All of this was prelude to the construction of the hotel, which began in the spring of 1914. Once again, the large lobby timbers for the hotel came from Washington and Oregon. They were shipped by rail to Browning (12 miles east of East Glacier) where they were then freighted by wagons on the road north to Babb. This road was considerably flatter and avoided the mud bogs of the road from East Glacier to St. Mary. The smaller timbers for the hotel were cut in the surrounding area. Hill built a sawmill and planing mill on site to prepare the logs for the hotel. The main four-story hotel structure consisting of 162 rooms was opened on July 4, 1915. "In 1917 the Many Glacier Hotel annex was added so that the hotel buildings followed the shoreline a total of 900 feet to the south."[15] The annex added another eighty rooms to the complex.

> The most striking feature of Many's original décor was the Circular Staircase. Standing in the lobby, near the front of the ... gift shop, it led downstairs ... The staircase included two semicircular flights of stairs, with beveled handrails. In the center was a fountain: a tall mound of native rocks and ferns, surrounded by a pool full of trout.[16]

The circular staircase was removed in 1957 so that the gift shop could be expanded over that space. In 2016, the National Park Service began a major rehabilitation of the hotel, which included reconstructing the circular staircase.

In the 1920s, National Park Service Director Stephen Mather was appalled by the sight of the sawmill next to the hotel. He warned Louis Hill several times to get rid of it. Hill never complied, and in 1925, while visiting Many Glacier, Mather took

Above: Tour buses and passengers are gathered at the front of Glacier Park Lodge in this undated T. J. Hileman photograph. It must be the early 1930s, as none of the 1936 third-generation buses are shown. Blackfeet Indians in headdresses are greeting the first bus. (*NPS GLAC8243*)

Below: Third-generation White Motor Company Model 706 buses are shown in front of Glacier Park Lodge in this *c.* 1940 photograph by T. J. Hileman. The first vehicle is a touring car used to transport V.I.P. guests from the train station. Blackfeet Indians gather near the second bus. (*NPS GLAC HPF1035*)

matters into his own hands. Stating "We don't have sawmills in national parks," he had several sticks of dynamite placed around the building and blew it up.[17] To this, Great Northern Railway vice-president William Kenney responded, "It was the most high handed, unwarranted and illogical thing that has probably ever occurred in any park, and committed by a government official, is particularly deplorable."[18] Despite this bluster, the sawmill was gone.

The Heaven's Peak fire of August 30, 1936, came roaring over Swiftcurrent Pass from the west, and fanned by high winds, it took direct aim at the Many Glacier Hotel. In its path, it destroyed thirty-three of fifty-four cabins that had been built near the Swiftcurrent Campground and all but two of the Many Glacier chalets. The hotel was saved when the fire diverted around Swiftcurrent Lake, sparing the hotel on the east end of the lake. Hotel employees manned fire hoses and kept watering the hotel down as fiery embers landed on the roof. It was an all-night battle, but they saved the hotel.

All Glacier Park Inc. and Glacier Park Transport Company employees from the 1960s to 1983 were hired by Ian B. Tippet, who was the manager of the Many Glacier Hotel as well as the personnel director. Tippet was a native of Devonshire, England, and a graduate of the London University Westminster College, where he studied hotel management. He obtained a Hilton Hotel scholarship to train at their hotel in Minneapolis, and it was there that he learned of the Great Northern Railway and Glacier National Park. He was hired as assistant manager at Glacier Park Lodge in 1955.

In 1960, the Great Northern Railway sold the hotels and transport company to Don Hummel's Glacier Park Inc., and they hired Tippet to become manager of the Many Glacier Hotel and personnel director for all the hotels and transport company. Over the years, Tippet hired thousands of college students to work in Glacier in the summer, recruiting music, drama, and instrument majors to work at Many Glacier to perform in musicals and dramas there. He hired geology and history majors to drive the buses and give informative tours. Every employee hired by Mr. Tippet, including this author, owes him a lifetime debt of gratitude for bringing us to the glories of Glacier for a summer. We mourned his passing on March 9, 2020. His musical productions truly helped Many Glacier Hotel live up to its reputation as the "Showplace of the Rockies."

To the north of Glacier, Canadian settlers around Waterton Lake recognized the importance of preserving the scenic beauty of the area. They petitioned the Canadian government for protection of the area, and on May 30, 1895, 54 sq. miles of land around the Waterton Lakes was set aside as Kootenay Lakes Forest Park.[19] It became Waterton Lakes National Park in 1911, and today contains 203 sq. miles. Louis Hill first visited Waterton in 1913 at the suggestion of a Canadian hiking companion he met while hiking in the Swiftcurrent Valley. Hill decided that the knobby hill overlooking the main Waterton Lake to the south would be a perfect spot for a hotel. Thus, the seed was planted for the future Prince of Wales Hotel. World War I intervened, however, and construction of the hotel did not begin until 1926, with an opening on July 25, 1927.

"That an American railway company would put up a single hotel in a Canadian national park is one of the many unique facts about the Prince of Wales Hotel."[20] Other unique facts include that the hill is often buffeted by extremely high winds, sometimes reaching speeds of 90 miles per hour, causing 12-foot-high wave crests on the lake. During construction of the hotel, one such gust of wind blew the hotel 3 inches off plumb, and the structure had to be winched back in place. One favorite jammer joke is

Above: Three red buses head west along Lake Sherburne toward the Many Glacier Hotel at the far end of the valley, *c.* 1950. In the dead center of the photo, Grinnell Glacier can be seen. Just to the right of the glacier is Grinnell Point, which towers above Swiftcurrent Lake and the hotel. (*Photograph by Fred Noble for the Great Northern Railway, NPS GLAC_11104*)

Left: This red bus is headed east from Many Glacier with Grinnell Point directly behind it. The jammer has apparently stopped to let the passengers view the wildflowers. (*Photograph by Bob Spring for the Great Northern Railway, NPS GLAC_11012a*)

This T. J. Hileman photograph, *c.* 1940, shows eight White Motor Company Model 706 tour buses lined up in front of the Many Glacier Hotel. Mount Gould rises directly behind the hotel with Gem Glacier in the notch to its right. (*NPS GLAC11295*)

Nine red buses line up in front of Many Glacier Hotel in this *c.* 1955 publicity photo for the Great Northern Railway. Six buses are backed up to the hotel and three are parked parallel to it. (*NPS GLAC_11047*)

Above: These red buses were parked on the shore of Swiftcurrent Lake on the evening of August 10, 1992. Many Glacier Hotel is just off the left side of the photograph. The bus tours never picked up passengers from this side of the hotel, so this must have been a V.I.P. tour or a pose for a publicity photo. (*Photograph by the author*)

Left: The sign says it all. (*Photograph by the author, July 25, 2012*)

that there is so much wind at the Prince of Wales Hotel that there are white caps on the water in the toilet bowls.

The hotel is named after Edward, the Prince of Wales, who visited the area in 1919 and bought the E. P. Ranch, which he owned for forty years. He became King Edward VIII, and then duke of Windsor after his abdication of the throne in 1936 when he married American divorcee Wallis Simpson. The hotel itself "is a solitary building with 90 guest rooms contained in seven stories under a steeply sloped roof capped by a 30-foot tower."[21] "The main building cost $371,000, with another $300,000 spent on the water tower, boilers and laundry and staff dormitories."[22]

One final unique fact is that Prohibition, which began in 1920, likely played at least a small part in the Great Northern Railway's decision to build the hotel to cater to thirsty Americans. American travelers could ride the red buses from Glacier Park Lodge, to Many Glacier Hotel, and then on to the Prince of Wales Hotel in Canada, where they could legally imbibe alcohol since the province of Alberta did not have Prohibition. This advantage for the railway did not last long, however, since Prohibition ended in 1933, and then the Great Depression set in. The hotel was closed from 1933 until 1936.

As the Depression became a stark reality in 1931, the Rotary Clubs of Montana and Alberta, Canada, met together to come up with a plan to promote the Waterton-Glacier area. The plan transformed into the Waterton-Glacier International Peace Park, which became a reality in 1933 when agreed to by both the American and Canadian governments. Though a passport is required to travel between the two parks today, the Prince of Wales Hotel "is the most visible reminder of the symbolic unity of the ... Peace Park."[23]

While the Prince of Wales Hotel is unique as an American hotel in a Canadian national park, Lake McDonald Hotel is unique in Glacier National Park in that it was not built by the Great Northern Railway, nor is the hotel that visitors see today the original hotel on the site. The original hotel was built by George Snyder in 1895. Snyder was one of the first settlers at the head of Lake McDonald. As the Great Northern brought more and more tourists to Belton, Snyder built his two-story frame hotel to accommodate them. The hotel had twelve rooms and faced 10-mile long Lake McDonald. "Since there was no road to Snyder's Hotel, he and Frank Kelly purchased a forty-foot steamboat, the *F.I. Whitney*, and had it hauled by rail and over trail to Lake McDonald from Flathead Lake."[24] Adventurous visitors got off the Great Northern at Belton, climbed on a stagecoach for the very rough ride on the road from Belton to Apgar, and then boarded the steamship for the voyage to Snyder's hotel. Snyder sold the hotel to John and Olive Lewis in 1906 for $1,500, and they renamed it the Glacier Hotel. The next year, Lewis built thirteen cabins along the lakeshore, which are still in use today.

When Glacier became a national park in 1910, John Lewis realized that he would need a larger hotel to accommodate visitors. He moved the two-story Snyder Hotel behind the site where he would build the new hotel, and he turned it into a general store. Construction of the new hotel began in 1913 with building supplies brought in by boat across Lake McDonald in the summer, and then across the frozen lake on sled in the winter. The new three-story "Lewis Glacier Hotel" opened for business on June 14, 1914, with sixty-five rooms.

Before Glacier became a national park, Lewis was involved in hunting and the fur trade. Many of his trophy heads and animal skins still adorn the walls of the hotel lobby.

Above left: A red bus pauses at the Chief Mountain overlook on its way to Canada and the Prince of Wales Hotel in June 1972. (*Photograph by the author*)

Above right: The south (lake-facing) side of the Prince of Wales Hotel, July 2012. The water tower can be seen just left of the roof. (*Photograph by the author*)

Below: One of the first White tour buses is parked next to the Belton Chalet, *c.* 1915. Following the plant trellises to the right is a path leading to the Belton train station, Great Northern's drop-off point for visitors to the west side of Glacier. (*Photograph by R. E. Marble, NPS GLAC6101*)

Headed by bus number 101, nine White model 706 buses are lined up at Belton Station in the late 1930s to receive passengers from the Empire Builder. (*Author's collection*)

In the winter of 1914, supplies for building the new Lewis Glacier Hotel were hauled by sled across a frozen Lake McDonald. (*Photograph by R. E. Marble, NPS GLAC5964*)

The fireplace in the lobby is massive—it is 20 feet wide, 12 feet deep, and 17 feet tall. On chilly mornings and evenings, several visitors are usually clustered inside the fireplace for warmth. Visitors could only reach the hotel by boat until 1920, when the road was finally completed between Apgar and the hotel.

> [In 1930] the Great Northern purchased Lewis's hotel, its furnishings, and surrounding land through a subsidiary ... In 1932, after discussions with the federal government, the railway sold the hotel and 285 acres to the National Park Service for half the $225,000 purchase price in return for a twenty-year lease on the facilities...Great Northern officials renamed the facility Lake McDonald Hotel.[25]

The hotel still stands today as part of the Lake McDonald Lodge complex, which also includes the cabins, camp store, and coffee shop. It is a major destination on the red bus tours of Glacier National Park.

The front side of Lake McDonald Hotel faces the lake because visitors could only reach the hotel by boat until 1920, when the road from Apgar to the other side of the hotel was finished. (*Photograph by the author, July 2012*)

Red buses are parked on the back side (away from the lake) at Lake McDonald Hotel in July 2012. This became the new entrance for visitors when the road to the hotel was completed in 1920. The massive fireplace of the hotel is inside, below the white chimney. (*Photograph by the author*)

Historical Spotlight: Red Bus Jamming in 1972 and 1973

To give a historical glimpse into the operation of the red buses and their service to the hotels, I would like to relate my experiences as the operator of red bus number 97 during the summers of 1972 and 1973. After graduating from the University of Nebraska in May 1972, I drove my orange Volkswagen Beetle to Glacier. Jammers were required to be twenty-one years of age and have previous bus or truck driving experience. I had driven a lumber delivery truck in Omaha the previous summers, so I qualified. A state chauffeur's license was required, but Nebraska did not have one at that time, so I was allowed to drive on my standard license.

As employees of the Glacier Park Transport Company, jammers were allowed to drive our private cars to Glacier, while the Glacier Park Inc. employees under twenty-one were required to arrive by public transportation, many arriving on Amtrak at East Glacier or Belton. The jammers did have their own dormitory building in East Glacier with private rooms. This was a luxury that we deeply appreciated, and it earned the jealousy of the other employees. Strangely though, the dorm was not heated, and it was plenty cold in the early days of June.

Our training began as soon as we arrived. We were given Donald Robinson's book *Through the Years In Glacier National Park* and told to memorize it for our tours. So, we sat around in the dorm lounge trying to keep warm while reading the book. We were each assigned a red bus for the summer and given general advice about care and upkeep of the bus by the attendant in the bus garage. We were assigned a trainer who would check our driving skills on a test drive from East Glacier to Two Medicine. That first drive over the winding mountain road was nerve-wracking indeed, but we soon became familiar with how the bus handled. The first week was filled with study, practice driving, and sample tours given by experienced drivers and transport agents.

Each hotel had a transportation agent who was responsible for assigning drivers to tours for the day and greeting buses as they entered the hotel driveway. Our lead trainer was Paul Meierding, who was the transportation agent at Many Glacier Hotel. Paul gave the tour to a bus full of new jammers over the roads of Glacier, pointing out the sights and describing the history and geology of the park. I took notes furiously as he was giving the tours. When it came time to give my first tour, I was as prepared as I could possibly be. Learning about the vast lore of history and geology of Glacier was a continual process throughout the summer. Eventually, all the jammers developed a tour spiel that they could practically give in their sleep.

I do not specifically recall my first tour, but it was probably from East Glacier to Many Glacier. The Going-to-the-Sun Road over Logan Pass often did not open until late June due to the heavy snowfall there, so our tours were limited to the east side run, or the southwest run to Lake McDonald. The tour to Many Glacier took about two hours, so if we left East Glacier at 10 a.m., we would reach Many by noon so that the passengers could have lunch there. After lunch, some tours continued to the Prince of Wales Hotel in Canada.

Alternately, drivers had the afternoon off, or we drove a different group of passengers from Many Glacier to East Glacier. The drive to Lake McDonald Lodge from East Glacier was about ninety minutes, so those tours also left East at about 10 a.m. Once Logan Pass opened for the season, my favorite tour was the one departing from Many Glacier, driving the Going-to-the-Sun Road over Logan Pass to Lake McDonald, or *vice versa*.

In the 1970s, the red bus tours were only offered between the four Glacier Park Inc. hotels: Glacier Park Lodge, Many Glacier Hotel, Prince of Wales Hotel, and Lake McDonald Lodge. Large tour buses were not allowed to drive over Logan Pass, so all the tour companies had to unload their passengers at the GPI hotels to be transferred to the red buses. We carried both the tour passengers and "regulars" (regs) on our tours. The regs were folks who had driven their cars to Glacier but wanted the experience of a red bus ride over Logan Pass. The regs and tour passengers were usually not mixed on the red buses, but occasionally, regs did ride if there were empty seats. As jammers, we preferred to take loads of tour passengers because they usually tipped better than regs. However, regs were often the more congenial passengers.

A jammer's life was a roving one in the 1970s. We rarely returned to the same hotel we started from on any particular day. Each hotel had a dormitory where the jammers stayed overnight. Only at East Glacier did we have private rooms in an exclusive jammer dorm. At Many Glacier, jammers bunked in one room on the top floor of the men's dormitory which was up the hill from the hotel. Six bunk beds in the room could accommodate twelve jammers. This was absolutely the worst place for jammers. It was crowded, hot, and impossible to get decent sleep in that room. Many jammers took to removing a mattress from a bunk bed and taking it out to their bus, where they placed

Above left: The road from St. Mary to Going-to-the-Sun Chalets opened in 1924. Here, five second-generation White buses motor eastward above the shore of St. Mary Lake, *c.* 1930. (*Photograph by T. J. Hileman, NPS GLAC3082*)

Above right: At the same spot as the previous photograph, three red buses head east along St. Mary Lake, *c.* 1950. The road has been greatly improved since 1930. (*Great Northern Railway publicity photo, NPS GLAC_11048*)

Below: A solitary red bus heads west over the Going-to-the-Sun Road along St. Mary Lake in August 1941. Due to World War II, no red bus tours occurred in 1943, 1944, or 1945. (*Photograph by Marion Post Wolcott, Library of Congress LC-USF34-058120-D*)

Above left: T. J. Hileman captured this photograph of nine red buses at Sun Point in 1940. Near this spot, the Going-to-the-Sun Chalets served visitors from 1913 until they were demolished in 1948. (*NPS GLAC10587*)

Above right: Nine red buses disembark passengers for a stroll at Logan Pass in this 1940 photograph by T. J. Hileman. (*NPS GLAC10096*)

Below: A red bus, a yellow snowplow, and several cars are parked at Logan Pass, *c.* 1950, in this photograph by Russell Bull for the Great Northern Railway. Mount Clements rises in the background. (*NPS GLAC_11133a*)

Above left: The author (left) and his brother, David Butler, pose on the hood of the author's red bus number 97 at Logan Pass in July 1972. (*Author's collection*)

Above right: Two of the new White Bus Model 706 drive down from Logan Pass heading west to Lake McDonald in 1936 on the Going-to-the-Sun Road. Mount Oberlin dominates the scene at top right. (*Photograph by T. J. Hileman, NPS GLAC HPF3986*)

the mattress in the luggage area at the back, and they slept under the stars with the bus canvas roof rolled back. I never did that. I figured that Glacier Park Inc. was obligated to provide a decent place for us to sleep. I did have many sleepless nights in that awful room at Many Glacier, though.

At Lake McDonald, there was a separate small dorm for the jammers, but it was a weird arrangement with bunk beds lining an open hallway, which led to the bathroom and showers in the middle of the building. Jammers walked through the hallway past the bunks at all times of the night to the bathroom, again ensuring a fairly sleepless night. Sometimes, there were as many as sixteen jammers staying overnight at Lake McDonald and the dorm could only sleep twelve. Luckily, a couple of times on those overcrowded nights, I was allowed to sleep in one of the unoccupied guest cabins. The Prince of Wales Hotel had a men's dormitory with one room assigned to jammers. I believe there were only four or six beds in this room, but there were seldom that many jammers spending the night at the Prince. When we eventually made it back to East Glacier, we collapsed in the peace and quiet of our own room.

Meals were provided at each hotel for the jammers, and we each had our favorite spots. The Many Glacier employee cafeteria usually served the best food, so that made up somewhat for the lousy dorm room there. The Lake McDonald and Glacier Park Lodge cafeterias were both good, not great. The Prince of Wales cafeteria was absolutely the worst. It was so bad that most jammers walked to downtown Waterton and paid for meals in a restaurant there. This was unfortunate because it was otherwise a beautiful experience to be in Canada. We looked forward to our seldom day off in

Canada because there was so much to do. It was always fun to tour the quaint shops in Waterton. Great hiking was available by taking the boat across the lake to the Boundary Trail on the west shore, the Crypt Lake Trail on the east, and the Goat Haunt trails on the south. In fact, we enjoyed hiking wherever we had a day off. Many Glacier had the most trails available, but great trails were available from all the hotels. Glacier Park Lodge even had a nine-hole golf course, which employees could play if there were no guests waiting on the first tee.

Toward the end of each summer, the jammers held a steak fry at the East Glacier dorm. Getting us all together was tricky because most tours for the day did not end up at East Glacier. The Transport Company allowed us to deadhead our buses to East Glacier from wherever our tours ended that day. If we had a girlfriend employee at one of the hotels, we were allowed to bring her along in the bus also. It was a great party, and most jammers deadheaded back to their original location late that night or very early the next morning after a few hours' sleep. Driving a red bus in Glacier National Park for the summer was the experience of a lifetime and I will always be grateful that I had the opportunity to do it for two summers. "Once a jammer, always a jammer!"

Above left: Employees were always playing pranks upon each other over the summer. Here, the author discovered that some enthusiastic female employees at Lake McDonald had decorated his bus with toilet paper. (*Author's collection, summer 1972*)

Above right: One morning at Glacier Park Lodge in the summer of 1972, the author found that Mr. Potato Head (looking suspiciously like the author) had mysteriously appeared atop the radiator on bus 97. Notice the White Motor Company insignia just below the potato. (*Photograph by the author*)

Jammers, transportation agents, and girlfriends overload a red bus at the annual jammer steak fry at East Glacier on August 12, 1972. (*Author's collection*)

Red buses are lined up outside the Transportation Garage at East Glacier in the summer of 1974. Jammers parked their buses overnight here, and then drove over to the driveway at Glacier Park Lodge for tour departures in the morning. (*Photograph by David Butler*)

3

HORSES TO THE CHALETS

Popular contemporary novelist Mary Roberts Rinehart rode through Glacier National Park in 1915 with a saddle horse group and wrote:

> The Great Northern has built huge hotels in three places, and at a dozen other locations has built groups of log houses, Swiss fashion, so that it is possible to follow the trails by day and to be comfortably housed and fed each night.[1]

While her count was exaggerated (there were actually two hotels and nine chalets), she concisely summed up Louis Hill's plan to accommodate visitors from his Great Northern Railway.

> What is perhaps most amazing about the two major grand lodges and nine smaller chalets that Louis Hill built in Glacier National Park was not simply that they were built in some of the most difficult terrain imaginable, but they were all in service in the space of just five years.[2]

If visitors were so inclined, they could see the interior of Glacier National Park on horseback from east to west, by riding from Glacier Park Hotel to Two Medicine Chalets, to Cut Bank Chalets, to St. Mary Chalets, to Going-to-the-Sun Chalets, to Many Glacier Chalets, to Granite Park Chalets, to Gunsight Chalets, to Sperry Chalets, and finally to the Lewis Hotel at Lake McDonald. It was then a boat ride across Lake McDonald to Apgar, and a stagecoach ride to the Belton Chalet at the Great Northern's western train station. Rather than such an exhaustive trip though, various circle rides usually lasting five days were set up between the chalets.

Well before Glacier became a national park in 1910, independent operators offered horse rides into the area from Apgar on the west and Midvale on the east.

> In 1911, after the park was established ... the first semi-permanent type of tent camps came into being, thereby enabling saddle horse parties to travel long distances through the park without having to set up camp each night.[3]

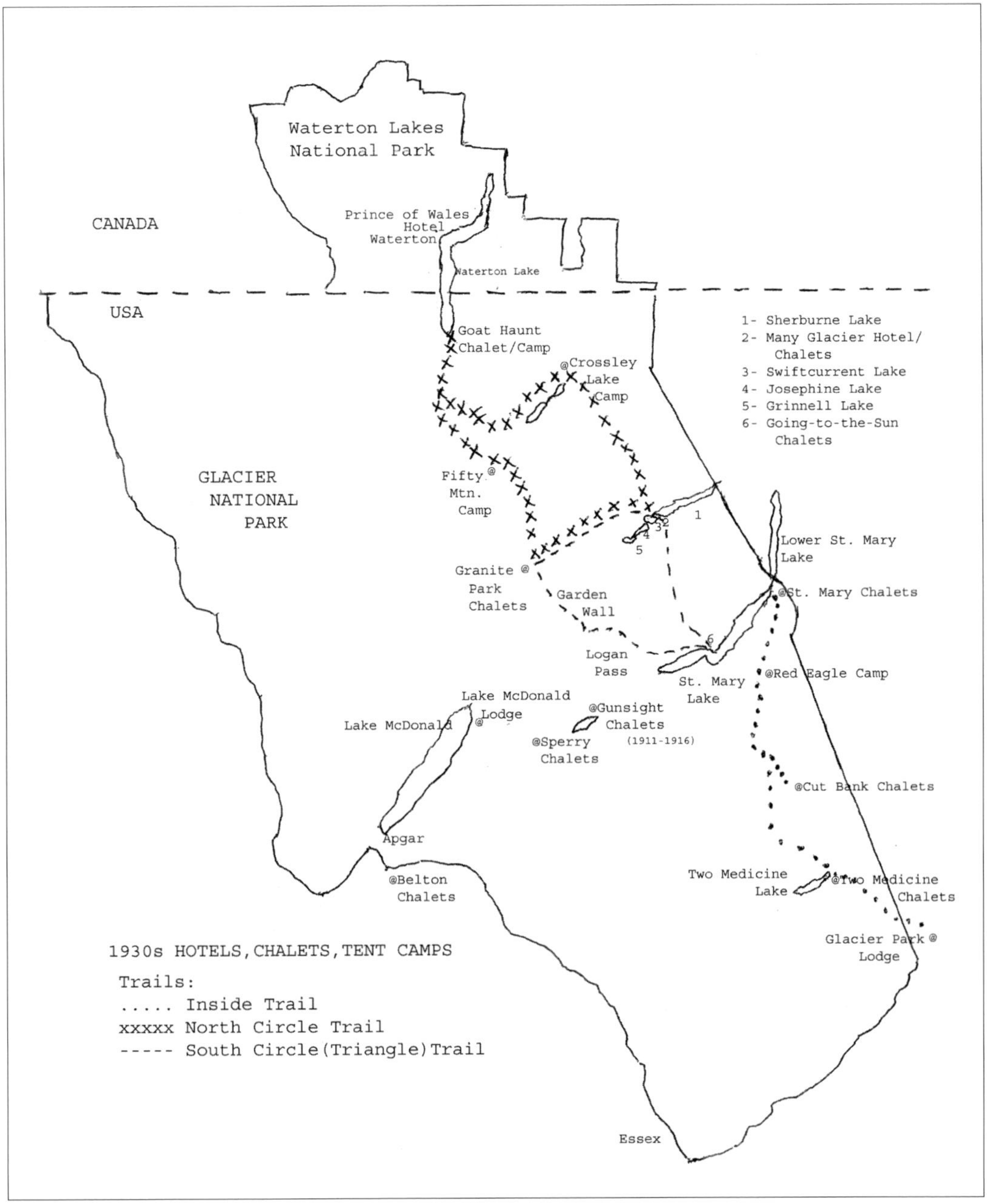

Glacier National Park hotels, chalets, tent camps, and connecting trails.

Above: Horseback riders on the trail along Sherburne Lake on the way west to Many Glacier, *c.* 1910. They may have been headed for an overnight stay at the primitive bunkhouse seen in the next photograph. (*Photograph by Fred Kiser, NPS GLAC7690*)

Below: Fred Kiser did not identify the location of this bunkhouse, which he photographed in Glacier in 1910. However, the mountain in the background appears to be Altyn Peak, originally called McDermott Peak. Early horseback riders may have stayed here overnight, before the tent camp and chalets at Many Glacier were built. (*Oregon Historical Society Library, ba021189*)

Above: This Fred Kiser photograph, *c.* 1910, shows the view the horseback riders would have seen as they came upon Lake McDermott (renamed Swiftcurrent Lake in 1928, although as author Jack Holterman pointed out, "It is hard to see how the name 'Swiftcurrent' can logically be applied to a lake"). The Many Glacier Hotel is yet to be built on the left shore of the lake and the chalets would rise on the lower right shore of the lake in 1913. (*NPS GLAC7691*)

Below: Fred Kiser photographed the newly constructed Many Glacier Chalets on the shore of Lake McDermott in 1913. The lake is visible just above the chalet on the left. Mt. Wilbur is the tall mountain in the center, and Swiftcurrent Peak rises in the distance to the left of Wilbur. (*Oregon Historical Society Library, ba020940*)

Louis Hill housed his laborers in these tent camps while the chalets were under construction nearby. He hired William and James Brewster out of Banff, Canada, to set up saddle horse operations between the tent camps and chalets. By 1915, Hill tired of the unreliability of the Brewster brothers' operation and turned over the horse concession to the recently formed Park Saddle Horse Company. The Brewster's stagecoach operations were also terminated and awarded to the Glacier Park Transportation Company with their new White buses.

> In 1915, under the leadership of W. N. Noffsinger ... a number of the small (horse) concessioners were combined as the Park Saddle Horse Company with their base ranch on the St. Mary River, several miles east of the park near Babb, Montana. This company then obtained a concession contract with the National Park Service and became the official saddle horse operator in the area.[4]

When W. N. Noffsinger died in 1924, his son George took over the operation of the Park Saddle Horse Company. He set up tent camps in the backcountry to accommodate riders on long rides between the chalets. In 1925, he established tent camps at Fifty Mountain, Goat Haunt, and Crossley Lake (named after an early park ranger named Joe Cosley, though his name was misspelled on maps). In 1926, he set up a tent camp at Red Eagle Lake. A Great Northern promotional brochure precisely described a tent camp:

> Here you eat meals that would do credit to an urban hotel although every pound of foodstuffs must be packed in on horseback,. You sleep in tents with painted board floors and side walls, and wood-burning heaters. The beds are good and blankets are plentiful. After dinner the host lights the big fire and he and the guides regale their guests with ... stories of the mountains and mountain men.[5]

With the establishment of the tent camps, the Park Saddle Horse Company could offer "Circle Tours" between the chalets and camps. The horse riders would never have to sleep on the ground or set up tents, and they had delicious meals every night.

The North Circle Tour began at the Many Glacier Hotel. The next night's stop was at Granite Park Chalets (the chalets were always referred to in the plural form in the early years), and then it was north to Fifty Mountain Camp and Goat Haunt Camp, heading back south to Crossley Lake Camp and then back to Many Glacier Hotel.

The South Circle Tour (also called the Triangle Tour) began at the Many Glacier Hotel with the first night's stop at the Going-to-the-Sun Chalets. The next night would be spent at Granite Park Chalets, with a return the following day to Many Glacier. A more extensive tour went from Going-to-the-Sun Chalets to Gunsight or Sperry Chalets, to Lake McDonald Hotel, to Granite Park Chalets, and back to Many Glacier.

The Inside Trail tour was also very popular. It began at Glacier Park Lodge, and went north to Two Medicine Chalets, Cut Bank Chalets, Red Eagle Camp, and finished at St. Mary Chalets. This tour could be extended, if desired, by boat on St. Mary Lake to Going-to-the-Sun Chalets, and then on to Many Glacier by horseback over Piegan Pass.

In the 1920s and 1930s, the saddle horse tours were so popular that the Park Saddle Horse Company was using 1,000 horses and accommodating 10,000 riders per summer. William J. Yenne, who worked in Glacier National Park for nearly thirty years as a horse

Above left: This *c.* 1950s scene shows the location of the Granite Park Chalets with a horse pack string being led and other horses grazing. The building on the left was the first chalet completed in 1914, while the building on the right was completed in 1915. Note the log "cribs" extending off the left side of the building. (*Photograph by Ira Spring for the Great Northern Railway, NPS GLAC_10826*)

Above right: This T. J. Hileman photograph shows the south end of the Goat Haunt Chalet, built in 1924 on Waterton Lake. The chalet was not built by the Great Northern Railway, but by a private investor from Waterton. It did not offer lodging, only meals and supplies. (*NPS GLAC10398*)

Below: Going-to-the-Sun Chalets (right) were located on a rocky cliff overlooking St. Mary Lake. The cabins seen on the isthmus extending into the lake were built by Louis Hill for his family. (*Photograph by George Grant on June 10, 1934, NPS Grant921*)

Above: Several buildings of the Going-to-the-Sun Chalets are seen on the cliffs of Sun Point above St. Mary Lake. Originally, the only way to reach the chalets was by boat from the St. Mary Chalets or by horseback. (*Photograph by T. J. Hileman, c. 1920s, NPS GLAC10191*)

Below: This *c.* 1940 publicity photograph for the Great Northern Railway shows one of the lodging buildings at Going-to-the-Sun Chalets. Going-to-the-Sun Mountain rises directly above the building. This group of chalets was the largest and most popular of the Great Northern chalets on the horseback Circle Tours. (*NPS GLAC_11069*)

Above: Ray Marble took this photograph of Gunsight Chalets on the shore of Gunsight Lake, *c.* 1914. Going-to-the-Sun Mountain rises in the distance. The chalets were about 11 miles from the Going-to-the-Sun Chalets, making a convenient overnight stop. Unfortunately, they were destroyed by an avalanche in 1916, necessitating riders to keep going another 4.5 miles to Sperry Chalets. (*NPS GLAC6090*)

Right: Guests relax on the porch and balcony at Sperry Chalets in 1939. The dining room is in a separate building behind this one. Mt. Edwards towers to the left. (*Photograph by T. J. Hileman, NPS GLAC8254*)

Above left: On July 16, 1932, the American flag flies over Two Medicine Chalets. The building on the right no longer exists. The building under the flag remains today and serves as a camp store. The chalets faced beautiful Two Medicine Lake and were conveniently located 12 miles north on the horse trail from Glacier Park Lodge. (*Photograph by George Grant on July 16, 1932, NPS GLAC11336*)

Above right: Cut Bank Chalets, seen in this *c.* 1925 T. J. Hileman photograph, were about 14 miles north of Two Medicine Chalets on the Inside Trail. Rising above the chalets is the spectacular, but ironically named, Bad Marriage Mountain. (*NPS GLAC10196*)

Below: St. Mary Chalets, *c.* 1914, on the shore of St. Mary Lake. The Chalets were the northern-most stop on the Inside Trail horseback tour, but travelers could venture on by boat or horse to the Going-to-the-Sun Chalets. (*Photograph by Ray Marble, NPS CLAC6180*)

Right: From the Going-to-the-Sun Chalets, riders would head north over Piegan Pass to the Many Glacier Hotel nearly 13 miles away. This *c.* 1932 T. J. Hileman photograph shows a lone rider at the pass with Mt. Gould on the left. (*NPS GLAC103003*)

Below: At the end of a long ride over Piegan Pass, riders could stay overnight comfortably at the Many Glacier Hotel, seen on the left shore of Swiftcurrent Lake. To the right of the bridge, several of the Many Glacier Chalets can be seen. (*Photograph by T. J. Hileman, c. 1930, NPS GLAC10290*)

packer on the backcountry trails for the National Park Service and then as supervisor of backcountry trails, wrote:

> The horse concession in Glacier National Park in the 1930s was a gigantic operation. Newspaper articles from big eastern papers, and stories in leading magazines proclaimed it the world's largest dude ranch, with hundreds of miles of scenic trails and tent camps ... At Many Glacier alone 300 horses were used, and there were times that even then they ran ... short of horses and guides ... Altogether, the Noffsinger horse concession , called the Bar-X-Six, had well over a thousand head of horses and employed over 125 people.[6]

The horse wrangler guides could be counted on telling whopper tales during the nightly campfires along the trail. One such guide was Jim Whilt, who recorded some of the stories in his book *Giggles from Glacier Guides*:

> So here in Glacier Park, God's own outdoors, God's and mine, myself and sixty others take the dudes over the trails and tell them some of the facts about this land of shining mountains for a period of three months. Then our work begins. We have to go over the entire park, shut off the waterfalls, fold up the switch-backs, brand all the young sheep and goats, dig all the dens for the bears, teach the little fish to swim and plant them in different lakes and streams.[7]

Bringing supplies in for the tent camps and chalets was quite an arduous chore for the horse packers. William J. Yenne described packing in supplies on the North Circle Tour:

> Some of the supplies for Goat Haunt Chalet, a part of the Noffsinger North Circle operation, were brought in by boat from Waterton Townsite in Alberta. Most however were packed all the way from Many Glacier by the North Circle Pack Strings, which also supplied Fifty mountain Camp and Granite Park Chalet. Supplies that reached Cosley Lake Camp by pack train from Many Glacier came by way of Red Gap Pass until the fall of 1931 when the trail past Ptarmigan Lake and through Ptarmigan Tunnel was made passable.[8]

The Ptarmigan Tunnel, completed late in 1930, is 183 feet long and 9 feet high, allowing pack horses and riders to easily pass through. It provided a more direct route to Crossley Lake, cutting off 6.5 miles from the Red Gap Pass Trail. Dr. Morton Elrod, a biology professor at Montana State University in charge of the Nature Guide Service in Glacier from 1922 to 1928, wrote about the attractions of Crossley Lake:

> This beautiful camp is located on the north shore of Crossley Lake, in the heart of a portion of the park that is quite unexplored. The setting is perfect, the mountains beautiful, the lake a lovely sheet of water, and full of fish. It is a place anyone can enjoy for days. Many tourists have discovered its charms, and loiter a week or more to fish, to roam, or to feast the eyes on the ever-changing mountains. Although the camp is in a wilderness, where all food and materials are brought in by pack horse, travelers have most of the comforts of civilized life, with excellent food.[9]

Excitement builds at Many Glacier Hotel as guests line up for their horses, *c.* 1931. The hotel was the locus of Park Saddle Horse Company tours, with rides to the south over Piegan Pass, west over Swiftcurrent Pass, or north over Red Gap Pass. (*Photograph by T. J. Hileman, NPS GLAC8248*)

George Grant photographed this horseback tour at the south portal of Ptarmigan Tunnel on July 23, 1932. Directly ahead of the group is Mt. Wilbur. The tunnel was completed in 1930 and opened in 1931. (*NPS GLAC11365*)

The Crossley Lake Camp had eighteen tent cabins. Bill Wanser worked there from 1924 to 1938. He described the tents and the dismantling of the camp at the end of each season:

> Each tent had a double bed, a ¾ bed, a small stove, wash basin, a portable potty, towels and bedding, all of which had to be carried to a permanent rat screen-lined "commisary" [*sic.*] building for permanent storage during the winter. Plus the dismantling of the main dining and kitchen tents, the laundry and the teepee.[10]

The popularity of the horseback tours began to fade with the increase of automobile travel to Glacier National Park and the opening of the Going-to-the-Sun Road in 1933. The road opened up the spectacular scenery in the heart of the park along the Continental Divide, which previously could only be seen on horseback or on foot.

When the park was closed in 1943 for World War II, the Park Saddle Horse Company ceased operations. After the war, the horse concession was split between operators at Lake McDonald, Many Glacier, and East Glacier. They operated essentially day trips, out and back, from the hotels, and those operations continue today. All the Great Northern chalets were completed by 1915 and they served horseback riders and hikers for thirty years. The chalets that offered overnight accommodation were all torn down after World War II (except Granite Park, Sperry, and Belton) due to deterioration and the declining popularity of horseback tours. The table below illustrates when the chalets were constructed, the total number of buildings, number of guests accommodated, and demolition date.

GLACIER NATIONAL PARK CHALETS

Chalet	Construction Dates	Number of Buildings	Number of Guests	Demolish Dates	Buildings Remaining
Belton	1909-1913	5	118		5
Two Medicine	1911-1913	5	100	1955-1956	2
Cut Bank	1912-1913	4	42	1948-1949	
St. Mary	1911-1913	7	150	1943	
Going-to-the-Sun	1912-1926	11	320	1948-1949	
Many Glacier	1913	8	32	1936	2
Goat Haunt	1924	2	0	1952	
Gunsight	1911	2	40	1916	
Sperry	1912-1914	2	48		2
Granite Park	1914-1915	2	34		2

All figures are approximate and are compiled from information found in the book Glacier's Historic Hotels and Chalets: Room With a View, by Ray Djuff and Chris Morrison.

Above: Crossley Lake Tent Camp bustles with activity in the early morning as wranglers round up horses in the corral while riders watch from the fence rails, *c*. 1940. From here, it was on south to Many Glacier, or west and north to Goat Haunt. (*T. J. Hileman photograph, NPS GLAC_11085*)

Below: On July 25, 1932, George Grant photographed riders on the Stoney Indian Pass Trail, as they stopped to admire the wildflowers. (*NPS GLAC11372*)

Historical Spotlight: The Remaining Chalets: Belton, Sperry, and Granite Park

The first chalet built by the Great Northern Railway at Belton was not for backcountry travelers at all. It was essentially an entry hotel for Great Northern passengers departing at the Belton Station for the western part of Glacier National Park. This created a problem the railway soon recognized—passengers went directly into the park without stopping overnight at the chalet. It was never a moneymaker for the railway, and Great Northern sold it after World War II.

Belton chalet opened on June 27, 1910, with a three-story, ten-room hotel, with a dining room and kitchen. The next year, two cabins were added along with "a third structure known as 'The Studio' with a huge skylight, (and) the five-bedroom, 32-by-53 foot Studio was meant for the use of artists."[11]

For the 1913 season, a twenty-four-bedroom annex was added, to complete the facilities at Belton. The chalet was sold many times after World War II, until it was finally purchased in 1970 by Ross and Kay Luding, who used it as a base for their reservation system for Granite Park and Sperry Chalets. They owned it until 1997 when it was sold to a couple who restored the buildings and opened it up again for lodging. With the high increase of visitation to Glacier National Park today, this is much-prized lodging at the western entrance to the park.

Although each chalet built by the Great Northern Railway to serve backcountry guests had its own unique characteristics, they were all built in the Swiss chalet style using logs cut locally, except for Granite Park and Sperry, which were built with local stone since they were located above timberline. Great Northern builders used native stone quarried on site to build those chalets.

> Even as work was progressing on his grand hotels … Louis Hill was planning a series of chalets deep in the backcountry of Glacier National Park at locations that were—and still are—accessible only on foot or on horseback. The seeds for this scheme had been sown in Hill's imagination by Lyman Sperry … Sperry surveyed the Gunsight Pass Trail and gave Louis Hill suggestions for two backcountry lodges. A chalet at Gunsight Lake … was completed in 1911 and the Sperry Chalets, near Sperry Glacier opened in 1914.[12]

Of the two remaining backcountry chalets—Sperry and Granite Park—Sperry is much more isolated and difficult to reach. Hikers face a 6.7-mile uphill trek from Lake McDonald to Sperry with an elevation gain of 3,300 feet. The Gunsight Trail to Sperry from the Going-to-the-Sun Road is nearly 14 miles long and traverses climbs to Gunsight Pass and Lincoln Pass. Yet Sperry remains extremely popular with hikers due to its location near Sperry Glacier and gorgeous 360-degree views. Lyman Sperry's suggestion for a chalet here was quickly accepted by Louis Hill.

A tent camp was erected at Sperry in 1911 and 1912, serving both guests and builders. Construction of the dining hall building began in 1912, and it opened in 1913. Then construction of the two-story, twenty-four-bedroom dormitory building began, and it opened in 1914. Park Saddle Horse Company rides to the chalet began in 1915, and visitors could rest and recuperate before attempting the arduous 3.5-mile hike up to Sperry Glacier. Horses could not travel to the glacier because of a sheer rock wall that hikers ascended by a ladder. Later, steps were blasted into the rock wall so that hikers

Above: The kitchen and dining building at Sperry Chalet as seen by T. J. Hileman in 1939. This was the first building at Sperry; it was constructed in 1912 and opened in 1913. The stairs at the left lead to the dormitory building. (*NPS GLAC8254*)

Below: The dormitory building at Sperry Chalet photographed by T. J. Hileman, *c.* 1925. The Great Northern Railway constructed this building and placed the initials "GNRy" in white stone at the end of the building. It opened in 1914, and, except for the stone walls, it was destroyed by fire in 2017. It has been rebuilt and was scheduled to reopen in 2020. (*NPS GLAC8238*)

did not have to hang out precariously over the edge on the ladder. Still, the steps are very steep, and hikers hang onto a wire cable while climbing the steps.

Traffic to Sperry Chalet decreased during the Depression and the chalet was closed during World War II. As horseback tours all but ceased after the war, the Great Northern Railway became tired of losing money on the chalet and sold it, and Granite Park Chalet, to the National Park Service for $1 in 1954. The Park Service awarded a concession contract for both chalets to Ross and Kay Luding. Kay Luding remained as manager of Sperry Chalet for over thirty years, assisted by her niece, Beth Dunagan.

Beth recorded her remarkable experiences at Sperry in her book *Welcome to Sperry Chalet*. As hiker visitation to both Sperry and Granite Park Chalets increased, problems developed in the drinking water and wastewater systems. "In 1992 Granite Park and Sperry Chalets were closed by the National Park Service because they failed to meet current standards set forth by Congress in the Clean Water Act and the Safe Drinking Water Act."[13] Beth Dunagan wrote of her feelings about this disaster:

> "They were closed!" When I heard those words, my heart turned to stone. Lanny, Kay, and all those associated with the 1993 season immediately lost their jobs. The family lost our mission in life- to preserve the Chalet and serve others ... More importantly, the guests had lost a tradition and also new experiences to pass down to succeeding generations. The hotel, with its priceless historic and artistic value would be abandoned, left to the elements and to fate.[14]

The situation did look bleak for the chalets, but former employees and visitors rallied to the cause with the "Save The Chalets" campaign. Funds were raised for the repair of the critical systems. During the summer of 1995 renovations began at both Sperry and Granite Park. Granite Park opened in the summer of 1996, but with vastly different operations. Overnight visitation was limited to twenty guests, and meals were no longer served. Hikers had to bring in their own food and water. There was no running water at the Chalet. A composting toilet served the needs of hikers. Repairs at Sperry Chalet took much longer as plans were made to restore it to full operation with traditional guest services. It was supposed to open in 1997, but it did not happen then, or in 1998. Finally, in 1999, Sperry was set to reopen, but even then, exceptionally deep snowfall delayed the opening until July 22.

The trials and tribulations for Sperry Chalet did not end there. The Sprague Creek fire east of Lake McDonald was started by a lightning strike on August 10, 2017. The fire kept burning and was driven rapidly east toward Sperry by high winds. On August 31, a cloud of burning embers landed on the Sperry dormitory roof. "The 103-year old structure burned fiercely and was destroyed, leaving blackened stonework suggestive of London after the Blitz."[15]

When news of the destruction spread, hearts were broken across the country (including this author) as those of us who had visited Sperry mourned its loss. The stone walls of the building were left intact, however, and immediately cries were raised to rebuild the interior. The National Park Service supported rebuilding, as did Montana's congressional delegation and thousands of supporters around the country. Time was of the essence as winter would soon set in. Helicopter loads of timbers were flown to Sperry and a supporting timber framework to hold up the stone walls from the interior was in place when snow started falling in October. The only question was whether those walls would withstand the Montana winter. Miraculously, the walls were still standing next spring. Reconstruction of the interior began in 2018 and continued in 2019. The rebirth of Sperry Chalet dormitory is scheduled to occur in the summer of 2020.

Granite Park Chalet had its own experience with fire in August 1936. Lighting started a fire in the dense forest on the slopes of Heavens Peak, and brisk winds blew the fire east toward Granite Park. As the fire took direct aim at the Chalet, it miraculously parted around it, destroying only the two outhouses at the Chalet. The fire then burned over Swiftcurrent Pass, destroying the auto camp cabins at Swiftcurrent Campground and burning the chalets at Many Glacier, although the hotel was spared.

Granite Park Chalet is located on a shelf of lava rock (not granite) at a strategic location where three trails intersect. The Loop Trail comes up from the Going-to-the-Sun Road in a strenuous climb of 4.2 miles. The Highline Trail comes from Logan Pass, 7.6 miles away, and the Swiftcurrent Pass Trail comes from the Many Glacier area, also 7.6 miles away.

The first building at the Chalet was built in 1914 and it was a one-story stone building with six bedrooms that could sleep eighteen guests on bunk beds. The second building was completed in August 1915, also built of stone. It had the appearance of a Swiss chalet with its two stories, slanted roof, and balcony. It had a kitchen, dining room, and lobby on the first floor and eight guest rooms on the second floor. With its central location, this chalet was a favorite stopover on the Park Saddle Horse Company tours. In the mid-1920s, twelve log guest rooms known as "cribs" were added to the two-story building to accommodate more guests. "They were log sheds built as wings on either side of the main chalet."[16] The author recalls staying in a crib in 1969 with his parents and brother. The spartan furnishings consisted of beds, linens, and a metal bowl to carry outside to fill with ice-cold water from a faucet in a breezeway between cribs. The six log cribs on the north side had been destroyed by this time, and the six cribs on the south side were all that remained. Those cribs were demolished in the 1970s. As mentioned previously, Granite Park Chalet has not offered meal service since 1996.

In the late 1940s, a room and three meals could be had at Granite Park and Sperry Chalets for the grand sum of $9.25. The chalets are tremendously popular with hikers today, and reservations are very difficult to come by. If you are fortunate enough to secure a reservation, be prepared for sticker shock with the prices listed for the 2020 season: Sperry Chalet charges $237 per night (with three meals) for the first person and $159 for each additional person in the same room. Granite Park serves no meals and charges $115 per night for the first person, and $82 for each additional person in the same room, plus $25 per night per person if linen and bedding are supplied by the Chalet. Despite the charges, who would turn down the opportunity to stay in one of these historic chalets in the heart of Glacier's most spectacular scenery?

Above: Granite Park Chalet sits on a lava rock outcrop with an incredible view west to Heavens Peak. This was the second building on the site, which was finished in 1915. The lower floor has the kitchen/dining room, and the upper floor has eight guest rooms. (*Photograph by T. J. Hileman, c. 1925, NPS GLAC8252*)

Below left: The Highline Trail was completed in 1912, connecting Logan Pass with Granite Park. A horseback rider can be seen on the trail at lower right. The trail switchbacks upward (upper right) between Haystack Butte on the left and the Garden Wall on the right. (*Photograph by Fred Kiser, c. 1913, NPS GLAC11810*)

Below right: Guide "Blackie" Dillon loads a horse at Granite Park, *c.* 1956. Dillon worked for the Park Saddle Horse Company for many years and was supposedly fired by boss George Noffsinger every year for drunkenness and rowdiness. Yet he was hired back every year, and he carried on as a guide long after the demise of the Company. (*Photograph by Ira Spring for the Great Northern Railway, NPS GLAC_10825*)

4

Boats Across the Lakes

Few people realize today that when they step in a tour boat on one of Glacier National Park's lakes, they are entering a vessel that is most likely as old as the famous red jammer buses. In fact, a few are even older: the *Sinopah* on Two Medicine Lake was built in 1926, as was the *Little Chief* on St. Mary Lake; the *International* on Waterton Lake was completed in 1928; and the *DeSmet* on Lake McDonald was built in 1930. These boats, all built by "Captain Billy" Swanson, are so well-constructed and preserved that they are listed on the National Register of Historic Places.

Boats have always played a role in the history of Glacier, first as vessels of transportation between places without roads, and then later as tourist cruises. The first boats were rowboats that carried Great Northern Railway passengers from the station at Belton across the Middle Fork of the Flathead River from 1891 until a bridge was built across the river in 1897.

After the stagecoach ride to Apgar, passengers then boarded George Snyder's steamboat the *F.I. Whitney* in 1895 for the 10-mile ride on Lake McDonald to Snyder's hotel near the head of the lake. Then Frank Kelly got into the act in 1906, with his boats ferrying passengers up Lake McDonald from Apgar to his cabins north of Snyder Hotel. The first permitted concessioner in the new national park was indeed Frank Kelly, who was awarded a permit in 1911 to operate three boats on Lake McDonald, one of which, the *Ethel*, was built by Captain Billy Swanson.

Some 30 miles southwest of what would become Glacier National Park, there was a booming boat business on Flathead Lake (approx. 30 miles long and 16 miles wide) in the 1890s. It provided a transportation link between the two great competing railroads of the northwest—the Great Northern Railway and the Northern Pacific Railway. The Great Northern built a spur line from Columbia Falls to Somers at the north end of Flathead Lake, and the Northern Pacific built a spur from Missoula north to Polson at the south end of Flathead Lake. The Flathead Valley produced timber and a wide variety of agricultural goods that could be shipped across the lake and out at one of the two railheads.

> The use of wooden boats in Glacier National Park for transportation and tourism was a natural extension of the existing boat culture on nearby Flathead Lake ... Without

> the thriving boatbuilding and steam-freighting business on Flathead Lake so close to the future site of Glacier National Park, there may not have been such a fine collection of wooden vessels built for the park's burgeoning tourism industry.[1]

One of the finest boat builders on Flathead Lake was John William Swanson, who came to be known as "Captain Billy" Swanson. He was born in Pennsylvania in 1883 and moved to Seattle in 1898. In 1906, he moved to Kalispell where he began building boats.

> He earned a strong reputation as a master boat builder for the growing freight traffic running up and down Flathead Lake. He operated his own company, the Flathead Boat Construction and Transportation Company. While he may have built more, at least 11 documented boats constructed by Swanson plied the waters of Flathead Lake ... most were steamers used for hauling machinery and timber.[2]

When roads were constructed around Flathead Lake in the early 1900s, the steamship business steadily decreased in importance. Captain Billy turned his attention to the new national park just to the north, and in 1911 constructed the vessel *Ethel* for Frank Kelly's boat concession on Lake McDonald. In 1915, Captain Billy completed the remarkable feat of transporting one of his large Flathead Lake boats, the *City of Polson*, to Lake McDonald.

With a crew of six, he piloted the boat north up the Flathead River and then McDonald Creek to Lake McDonald. The arduous journey of nearly 60 miles over rocks and rapids took nearly two weeks to complete. The boat was drydocked at Lake McDonald, and 10 feet was added to its length so that it could transport over 100 passengers and baggage from Apgar to the head of Lake McDonald. It was renamed *Lewtana* and it was contracted out to Frank Kelly who used it through the summer of 1929.

On the east side of Glacier National Park, the Great Northern Railway's subsidiary Glacier Park Hotel Company was given a permit in 1912 to operate two boats on St. Mary Lake to ferry passengers between St. Mary Chalets and the Going-to-the-Sun Chalets. These two boats were the *Red Eagle* and the *Glacier*:

> [Each was] thirty-two feet long and with a capacity of twenty-five persons each ... In 1913 the *Red Eagle* was replaced by the *St. Mary*, a gas-powered boat sixty-four feet long with a fourteen-foot beam, capable of carrying seventy-five passengers from St. Mary to Sun Camp.[3]

The *St. Mary* was retired in 1933 with the opening of the Going-to-the-Sun Road.

Beginning in 1912, the Hotel Company also operated boats on Two Medicine Lake and rented rowboats at Many Glacier on Lake McDermott (renamed Swiftcurrent Lake in 1928). In 1916, the Hotel Company contracted the boat business out to Captain Billy Swanson. In 1920, Swanson won the concession contract for these lakes and took over the boats from the Hotel Company. He then "went into a prolific period of boat-building, launching seven boats over the next decade."[4]

Swanson built three similarly designed 36-foot vessels, the first of which, the *Wymufus*, was for Two Medicine Lake, and the other two destined to be the first boats on Many Glacier's lakes, with the *Josephine* going to Lake Josephine and the

T. J. Hileman photographed *St. Mary* at the boat dock at the St. Mary Chalets, *c.* 1925. Passengers were ferried from here to the Going-to-the-Sun Chalets. (*NPS GLAC5227*)

The launch *St. Mary* at the Going-to-the-Sun Chalets, *c.* 1925. The porters had a steep climb with luggage up the rocky cliffs to the chalets. The *St. Mary* was launched on St. Mary Lake in 1913 with a capacity of seventy-five passengers. (*Photograph by T. J. Hileman, NPS GLAC8237*)

Grinnell going to Lake McDermott. In 1926, Swanson constructed and launched two new 45-foot, fifty-passenger boats—the *Rising Wolf* for his booming business on Two Medicine Lake and the *Little Chief* for St. Mary Lake.

In 1927, Swanson began construction of the launch *International* for the Glacier Park Hotel Company for use on Waterton Lake in conjunction with the Hotel Company's recently completed Prince of Wales Hotel at Waterton. Swanson built a boathouse at Goat Haunt at the south end of Waterton Lake, constructing the *International* there so that the boat would be registered in the United States rather than Canada.

> Besides catering to hotel guests and other visitors to Waterton ... Great Northern officials also envisioned the boat as part of horseback trip itineraries ... At Goat Haunt, the launch would whisk riders up the lake to the Prince of Wales Hotel for a restful night in luxurious accommodations.[5]

The *International*, launched in 1928, cost $24,000 to build. It was the largest of all the Glacier/Waterton launches. It was "seventy-three feet long with a sixteen-foot beam, carried two engines operating twin screws, and was capable of carrying 250 passengers."[6]

At Lake McDonald, the Going-to-the-Sun Road had been constructed as far as the Lewis Hotel (which replaced the Snyder Hotel) by 1921. This considerably reduced boat passenger traffic on Lake McDonald. In 1929, Captain Billy Swanson scuttled all the remaining concession boats on Lake McDonald at the end of the season. He then "completed the 56-ft. new passenger launch, *DeSmet*, at his shop in Kalispell in a mere six weeks, and transported it by truck to the park for the 1930 season."[7] In 1930, the National Park Service awarded the contract for the Lake McDonald boat service to the Glacier Park Transportation Company. The *DeSmet* still operates on Lake McDonald today, offering scenic cruises from the Lake McDonald (formerly Lewis) Hotel.

In 1933, Captain Billy Swanson continued his shipbuilding activity with the construction of the *Chief Two Guns*, a 45-foot, sixty passenger vessel to replace the *Grinnell* on Swiftcurrent Lake. By 1938, however, Swanson was ready to step back from his operations, and he sold all his boats and boathouses to Arthur Burch for $25,000. Burch then formed the Glacier Park Boat Company, which operated Glacier's boats for the next eighty years.

Over the years, Glacier's boat concessions have been a confusing tangle of operators, with the constants being Captain Billy Swanson and then the Arthur Burch family.

> Of all the park concessions, the boat operators present[ed] the most confusing picture, particularly during the 1920s, with different companies, including the hotel company, operating on different lakes, and many of the operations were to change hands.[8]

By 1946, there were three major boat operators in Glacier: Glacier Park Boat Company (Arthur Burch) operating boats on the east side lakes; Glacier Park Hotel Company operating the *International* on Waterton Lake; and the Glacier Park Transportation Company operating the *DeSmet* on Lake McDonald. Eventually, all the boats came under the control of the Glacier Park Boat Company.

In 1926, Captain Billy Swanson constructed the *Rising Wolf* to use in conjunction with the *Wymufus* for passengers on Two Medicine Lake. This George Grant photograph from July 16, 1932, shows Sinopah Mountain rising above Two Medicine Lake and reflected on it. (*NPS GLAC11343*)

George Grant photographed the boat dock at Two Medicine Lake on July 16, 1932. The *Rising Wolf* is docked on the left side with several rowboats on the right side. Sinopah Mountain rises prominently on the left. (*NPS GLAC11339*)

Above: On July 16, 1932, the *Rising Wolf* is docked on Two Medicine Lake with the Two Medicine Chalets lining the shore. (*Photograph by George Grant, NPS GLAC11335*)

Below left: The sightseeing boat *Sinopah* cruises on Two Medicine Lake, *c.* 1956. This boat was originally constructed by Captain Billy Swanson in 1926 and named the *Little Chief*, where it operated on St. Mary Lake. It was later moved to Two Medicine Lake and renamed *Sinopah*. It still cruises there today. (*Photograph by Ira Spring for the Great Northern Railway, NPS GLAC_10812*)

Below right: The launch *International* is docked on Waterton Lake, *c.* 1960. The Prince of Wales Hotel is on the hill above the boat. The *International* was constructed by Captain Billy Swanson in 1927 and launched in 1928. (*Photograph by Walt Dyke for the Great Northern Railway, NPS GLAC_10956*)

Above left: The launch *International* cruises on Waterton Lake, *c.* 1960. The view is north toward Waterton Township in Canada. (*Photograph by Walt Dyke for the Great Northern Railway, NPS* GLAC_10980)

Above right: The *International* is docked in Waterton in the summer of 1972. At this time, it was owned by Glacier Park Inc. The view is south toward the spectacular peaks of Glacier National Park, Montana. (*Photograph by the author*)

Below: A motorboat cruises past the *DeSmet* on Lake McDonald in 1953. Captain Billy Swanson built the *DeSmet* and launched it on Lake McDonald in 1930, where it still cruises today. Mt. Cannon rises just to the left of the flagpole. (*Photograph by Ira Spring for the Great Northern Railway, NPS GLAC_11035*)

On 4 July 1933, George Grant photographed the sightseeing boat *Chief Two Guns*, unloading passengers at the dock on Swiftcurrent Lake in front of the Many Glacier Hotel. Grinnell Point rises across the lake. The *Chief Two Guns* was built by Captain Billy Swanson in 1933. (*NPS GLAC11303*)

Swanson continued to provide guidance to Arthur Burch after the sale of the boats in 1938. In 1945, they collaborated on building the *Big Chief*, which ran on Swiftcurrent Lake from 1945 to 1961. Here is where things get very confusing. The *Chief Two Guns*, which had been running on Swiftcurrent Lake, was moved to Lake Josephine to replace the old launch *Josephine*. Thus, photographs show the *Chief Two Guns* on both Swiftcurrent Lake and Lake Josephine, however, at different time periods.

In 1961, the *Big Chief* was moved from Swiftcurrent Lake to Josephine Lake to replace the old *Chief Two Guns*, and the *Big Chief* was renamed the *Morning Eagle*. The *Morning Eagle* still operates on Lake Josephine today. Just to add to the confusion, Arthur Burch built a new boat for Swiftcurrent Lake in 1961 and named it *Chief Two Guns*. This boat still operates on Swiftcurrent Lake today. Rounding out the naming circus, the 1926 *Little Chief* on St. Mary Lake was moved to Two Medicine Lake and renamed the *Sinopah*, where it still operates today. The 1926 *Rising Wolf* from Two Medicine Lake ended up at St. Mary Lake after 1975, and it was renamed *Little Chief*, where it still operates today.

When the Great Northern Railway sold its concession operations in 1960 to Glacier Park Incorporated, the launch *International* went along with it. In 1975, Glacier Park

Horse guides meet the sightseeing boat *Chief Two Guns* on Lake Josephine. By the time of this photograph, *c.* 1953, the *Chief Two Guns* had been moved from Swiftcurrent Lake to Lake Josephine. (*Photograph by Ira Spring for the Great Northern Railway, NPS GLAC_11039*)

The *Chief Two Guns* docked on Lake Josephine, *c.* 1955. At this time, the launch *Big Chief* was operating on Swiftcurrent Lake. Passengers had to hike two-tenths of a mile over a hill between the two lakes to transfer from one boat to the other. Mt. Gould rises in the background. (*Photograph by Russell Bull for the Great Northern Railway, NPS GLAC_11140*)

Above left: In this 1965 photograph for the Great Northern Railway Public Relations Department, the new *Chief Two Guns* (built in 1961) cruises on Swiftcurrent Lake. Just above and a little to the right of the boat is the small hill that passengers must hike to get from Swiftcurrent Lake to Lake Josephine. (*NPS GLAC10886*)

Above right: The new *Chief Two Guns* built by Arthur Burch in 1961 cruises on Swiftcurrent Lake with Grinnell Point in the background, *c.* 1965. (*Great Northern Railway photograph, NPS GLAC_10914*)

Below: A group of tourists stands next to the new *Chief Two Guns* boat at the dock on Swiftcurrent Lake, *c.* 1965. Mt. Wilbur is in the background. (*Great Northern Railway photograph, NPS GLAC_11068*)

Incorporated sold the *International* to the Glacier Park Boat Company, which then operated it until 1985. In 1986, the Boat Company sold the *International* to Stan Kretz, a Calgary school principal who had operated tour boats on Waterton lake during his summer vacations since the 1950s. Today, Waterton Shoreline Cruises, the Kretz family business, continues to own and operate the *International.*

Throughout this convoluted history there was one constant—Captain Billy Swanson:

> [His] mark on the nascent Glacier National Park boating concession is undeniable. His legacy as the most prolific boat builder and recognition of his building skills within the Park helped jump-start the water-based industry and provided continuity and stability through the years. Swanson-constructed boats dominated the lakes of Glacier. His reputation and knowledge of boat-craft allowed him to build boats not only for his own concession, but also for concessions operated by other companies ... His designs display a mastery of mixing flowing lines and beautiful bright work with the stout construction necessary to meet the park's large glacial lakes and extreme weather.[9]

In 2019, the boat concession contract for Glacier National Park was once more put out to bid for a ten-year period beginning in 2020. This raised the huge question of what would happen to the historic Swanson boats if a company other than the Glacier Park Boat Company won the bid? No one knew, but a lot was at stake. In 2015, the Boat Company reported that 68,459 passengers rode the boats producing $1.4 million in revenue, and in 2017, 86,109 passengers produced $2.1 million in revenue.[10] Fortunately, the historic boat service will be preserved as the National Park Service on August 20, 2019, awarded the next ten-year contract to the Glacier Park Boat Company.

Historical Spotlight: Photographer George Alexander Grant

Several photographs in this chapter and throughout the book are by George Grant and T. J. Hileman. Both were "official" photographers in Glacier National Park, Hileman for the Great Northern Railway beginning in 1925 and Grant in 1929 for the National Park Service. Hileman is profiled in Chapter Six.

George Alexander Grant was the first chief photographer of the National Park Service, hired on April 8, 1929. He photographed Glacier National Park in 1932, 1933, 1934, 1940, 1941, and 1948. "Over the course of his twenty-five-year career with the Park Service, Grant visited more than a hundred parks and produced over thirty thousand images."[11] Grant met Hileman at least once, when he photographed Hileman filming for the Great Northern Railway at Piegan Pass in 1932.

Grant, like Hileman, was a native of Pennsylvania. He was born in Milton, PA, on March 4, 1891. Grant enlisted in the army in 1917 and was posted at Fort D.A. Russell near Cheyenne, Wyoming. It was here that Grant fell in love with the wide-open west. He became a seasonal ranger in Yellowstone National Park for the summer of 1922. He then returned to Pennsylvania, working on his photographic craft for Penn State University, until he was hired by Horace Albright, his former superintendent at Yellowstone, for the chief photographer position in 1929. He retired in 1954 when his position was eliminated due to Park Service budget cuts. He moved to Santa Fe, New

Mexico, in 1958 where he lived for most of the next six years until his death on October 11, 1964, at the Veterans Administration Hospital in Baltimore.

The enduring significance of George Grant's work was summed up by Montana naturalist and photographer George McFarland, who had met Grant late in his career:

> George Grant photographed to document that the West of the imagination was not all gone; that it still existed in the national parks and environs. His pictures furthermore showed that whether one was an outdoor expert or novice, there is a national park experience for everyone.[12]

The launch *St. Mary* is docked at the landing for St. Mary Chalets in this George Grant photograph from July 5, 1933. This would be the final year of operation for the *St. Mary*, which was retired at the end of the season due to loss of passengers to automobile traffic when the Going-to-the-Sun Road opened. (*NPS GLAC11385*)

5

Roads Around the Park

As convoluted as boat operations in Glacier National Park were over the years, the situation with roads around the park is much more straightforward. If one imagines Glacier's boundaries as an elongated box with roads along the top and bottom of the box, roads along the sides of the box, and one road across the middle of the box, it pretty well sums up the state of roads in the park today. On the east side of the box runs Montana Highway 49, which joins U.S. Highway 89. On the north side of the box is the Chief Mountain International Highway, which travels into Waterton Lakes National Park in Canada. On the south side of the box is U.S. Highway 2. On the west side of the box is Glacier Park Road 7, a gravel road that extends north to Bowman Lake and Kintla Lake, just a few miles south of Canada. Of course, across the center of the box is the world-famous Going-to-the-Sun Road, a paved wonder among the peaks and valleys of the park.

As we have seen, the first roads in Glacier were built by the enterprising settlers at the west end of Lake McDonald who needed a road connection to Belton to bring travelers from the Great Northern Railway to the vacation cabins at the lake.

> [This road] grew out of necessity rather than planning, and followed the path of least resistance (over which) buckboards bounced and plunged hauling visitors from the railroad depot to Apgar ... One must stretch his imagination to picture it as a road, according to present day standards. No grading was done, and no bridges were built. Corduroy—short pieces of log laid crosswise—was placed across the worst mud holes, and the necessary trees were cut to allow the wagons to pass.[1]

No road extended beyond Apgar, so boats brought travelers from Apgar to the hotel and cabins at the northeast end of Lake McDonald. When hotel owner John Lewis built a new hotel in 1914 at the head of the lake, he realized it would greatly benefit if there were a road to his hotel. So, Lewis set about building the road himself from 1919 to 1921, and it ended up being the eventual first leg of the Going-to-the-Sun Road.

Over on the east side of the park, road-building began:

> When the Great Northern Railway started to build its hotels and chalets ... they immediately ran into transportation difficulties. Tons of lumber and other building materials, boilers for heating plants, supplies and equipment of all kinds had to be hauled into these mountain valleys for the construction of these large hotels.[2]

If the Great Northern Railway wanted a road between the newly completed Glacier Park Lodge and the Many Glacier Hotel under construction to the north, they would have to build the road, as the new national park had no funds to do so. Thus, in 1911, the railway started construction of the road from Midvale (East Glacier) to Many Glacier. The road was completed by August 1913, and on August 7, Louis Hill and his party drove the first automobile over the road. While the road was well-graded, it was not surfaced, and we have seen the trouble the buses had traversing this road in the wet summer of 1915. Surfacing of the road did not begin until 1926 and was completed in 1929 when the road was extended all the way to the Canadian border, for a total of fifty miles from East Glacier to the border. The road became known as the "Blackfeet Highway" since it ran entirely through the Blackfeet Reservation.

Today, the road begins as Montana Highway 49 at East Glacier and becomes U.S. Highway 89 at Kiowa Junction. The high point of the road is 6,067 feet elevation at St. Mary Ridge (also known as the Hudson's Bay Divide), which extends east from Divide Mountain. Divide Mountain is named because waters from the north flow into Hudson's Bay, and waters to the south flow into the Gulf of Mexico. At Triple Divide Peak, a few miles southwest, a third "divide" is added as waters from the peak flow west to the Pacific Ocean. There are three westward road extensions off the Blackfeet Highway. The first is a 7-mile paved road into the Two Medicine Valley. Heading north, the next extension is the 6-mile gravel road into Cut Bank. At St. Mary, the Going-to-the-Sun Road joins the Blackfeet Highway. The final westward extension from the Blackfeet Highway is the 12-mile paved road from Babb to Many Glacier.

From Babb, U.S. Highway 89 continues northeast to the Canadian border and on to the town of Cardston, Alberta. From there, a road west leads to Waterton Lakes National Park. In 1932, with the agreement forming Waterton-Glacier International Peace Park, there was immediate pressure to shorten this circuitous route by building a road northwest from Babb (at Kennedy Creek) directly to Waterton, thus cutting about 25 miles off the journey. Immediate plans for the road were thwarted, however, when the Great Northern Railway announced it would not open the Prince of Wales Hotel in the summer of 1933:

> [This was due to] "business conditions which might make the operation of the hotel unprofitable" ... Couched in the announcement was the railway's desire to see the quick completion of the new road which was "bound to increase the flow of tourists from the United States to Waterton." It was corporate pressure at its most obvious: no road, no hotel operation.[3]

Construction of the road finally resumed in earnest in 1934. The "Canadian section was built in its entirety by unemployed relief workers under the auspices of the national park

George Grant photographed the Two Medicine checking station on July 17, 1932. Today, the road is paved for 7 miles from the Blackfeet Highway to Two Medicine Lake. Rising Wolf Mountain is in the background. (*NPS GLAC11327*)

Marion Post Wolcott photographed the road into Many Glacier in August 1941. Salamander and Grinnell Glaciers are seen in the center below the notch in the Garden Wall. Today, the road is paved for the 12 miles between Babb and Many Glacier. (*Library of Congress, LC-USF34-058058-D*)

On the Fourth of July 1933, this couple is enjoying the view of Swiftcurrent Lake from their automobile. The Many Glacier Hotel is at the left and Mount Gould and the Garden Wall are in the distance. (*Photograph by George Grant, NPS GLAC11304*)

service."[4] These workers became known at the "20 cent men" because as worker Frank Goble wrote: "The work was hard, the pay was small: 20 cents a day with board, room and work clothing supplied."[5] Work progressed on both sides of the border, and the road was opened on June 14, 1936. There are approximately 15 miles of road on each side of the border, and the highest point is at the international boundary at 5,329 feet above sea level. The road cuts through only about 5 miles of the very northeast corner of Glacier National Park. There was some initial discussion about what the name for the new road should be, but "Chief Mountain, with its many perspectives, can be seen for miles on three sides and is a regional landmark in both the U.S. and Canada."[6] Thus the consensus was that the appropriate name would be the "Chief Mountain International Highway."

With all this road construction on the east side of the park, there was still no way to get to the west side of the park by automobile. Prior to the completion of U.S. Highway 2 along the south boundary of the park in 1930, travel was not simple:

> To get an automobile across the divide it was necessary to have it loaded upon a flatcar at either East Glacier Park or West Glacier, to be ferried across the summit by freight

A highway crew plows the Chief Mountain International Highway on May 1, 2009, preparing to open the road for the summer season. Chief Mountain is at the top right. This view is from the U.S. side of the border. (*Unknown photographer, NPS*)

> train while its owner made the same trip in a passenger coach. This ferry service was provided by the Great Northern Railway, in proper season, for $12.50 per car.[7]

Highway 2 was opened for automobile traffic on July 19, 1930, and a dedication ceremony was held at Marias Pass on August 23. The highway was named the "Theodore Roosevelt Highway" in honor of President Roosevelt's tireless efforts for conservation of the forests of the United States. The highway parallels the railroad tracks and does not enter Glacier National Park except for about three miles at the southernmost tip of Glacier. The highway exits Glacier at Essex, where it rejoins the railroad tracks paralleling the Middle Fork of the Flathead River all the way to West Glacier. It is approximately 58 miles between East Glacier (elevation 4,796 feet) and West Glacier (elevation 3,200 feet) on Highway 2, with the high point at Marias Pass (5,213 feet).

On the west side of Glacier National Park, a road was built from Belton all the way north to Kintla Lake in 1901, due to a discovery of oil in that location. There was no restriction on mining activity before the area became a national park in 1910. This 42-mile gravel road (Glacier Park Road 7) lies entirely within the boundary of the park today. It is still gravel:

> This lack of modernization is by design, and the road is adequate for the needs of hikers, campers and fishermen who use it. In other words, the North Fork area is purposely without hotels, paved roads and other trappings of civilization in order that this section of the Park may the [*sic.*] better maintain its wilderness flavor and primitive appeal.[8]

Above left: U.S. Highway 2 crosses Marias Pass here and is seen at the base of the tall pine trees. The obelisk honors President Theodore Roosevelt, and the statue is of John Stevens, who discovered the pass for the Great Northern Railway. (*Photograph by the author, July 2012*)

Above right: This plaque on the obelisk monument at Marias Pass honors President Theodore Roosevelt for "his leadership in the conservation of the forests of the United States." U.S. Highway 2 is named the "Theodore Roosevelt Highway" in his honor. (*Photograph by the author, July 2012*)

Since the North Fork of the Flathead River forms the northwestern boundary of Glacier National Park, this is known as the "North Fork Road." Across the river to the west, there is a parallel road named "North Fork" in Flathead National Forest. In 1965, the Camas Creek Road of 11 miles was completed inside Glacier to connect Apgar with the Flathead Forest road. It also gives access to the 6-mile trail up Huckleberry Mountain to the fire lookout there.

With the completion of U.S. Highway 2 in 1930, automobiles could now get from the east side of Glacier National Park to the west side. However, there was still no road across the Continental Divide in the midsection of the park. A start had been made on such a road by John Lewis with the road he built along Lake McDonald to his hotel. From there, a road would have to go east up the McDonald Creek valley, climb the Garden Wall to Logan Pass, and then descend east around Piegan Mountain and

The southern entrance to the North Fork Road in 2017. The sign reads: "'Driving Glacier's North Fork Country'—Roads inside Glacier National Park's North Fork Country are maintained in a primitive condition. They are rough, dusty and narrow, with many blind curves and few pullouts. The maximum posted speed limit is 20 mph. Large RVs or long trailers may have difficulty traveling these roads. Please contact a Park Ranger for additional info." (*Photograph courtesy of "Magicpiano" from Wikipedia*)

Going-to-the-Sun Mountain to the shore of St. Mary Lake to the eastern boundary of the park. Going-to-the-Sun Mountain was named by early explorer James Willard Schultz, who either made up the name or based it on a Blackfeet legend (also possibly made up by Schultz), which posited that a Blackfeet god came down from the sky to help his people on earth, and when he was finished, he climbed back up this mountain to his home in the sun. At any rate, this name was also applied to the highway that was built.

> The Going-to-the-Sun Road is universally proclaimed as one of the great roads of the world. It skirts the shores of beautiful lakes, winds through deep cedar forests carpeted with ferns, passes lofty waterfalls and foaming cataracts, half-tunnels lofty cliffs, climbs gently but steadily above timber line to the meadows of alpine flowers on Logan Pass. It clings precariously to the Garden Wall, out of which it is hewn, yet is wide and safe with a strong protective guard-rail of stone constructed for miles along it. When it is opened for travel in June, it runs through canyons of snow a dozen or more feet deep, and a thousand crystal waterfalls cascade upon it.[9]

From the Lewis Hotel on Lake McDonald, the road was next extended 7 miles eastward to Avalanche Creek by 1924. Here, things came to a halt, as the best route up to Logan Pass was debated. One proposed route would climb the Garden Wall from here by a series of several switchbacks. This would cause severe scarring on the Garden Wall landscape though, and an alternate route was sought. In 1924, chief highway engineer Frank Kittredge was assigned the task of finding the alternate route. When survey work began in September 1924, Kittredge had trouble keeping men employed on the crew as he wrote:

> The daily climb of from 1,200 feet to 3,000 feet over cliffs and through brush proved too strenuous for many. Work on the line along the steep mountainside and cliffs proved too hazardous for those not adapted to such work. Working in the rain and sleet was beyond endurance for many more.[10]

When Kittredge's survey work was finally completed, only one switchback was necessary on the Garden Wall at a spot called the "Loop" where the road changed direction from northwest to southeast, looping back upon itself at a higher level. This was the most difficult section to build:

> [It was] roughly eight miles across the face of the Garden Wall from the ... Loop to Logan Pass. The work consisted of notching the roadway into the cliff and constructing stone retaining walls [on the outside]. Because of the heavy snowfall, the work was seasonal, limited mainly to the summer ... No major construction occurred on the Garden Wall in 1929 and 1930 because of the West Side Fire in 1929 and the Great Depression ... Despite the difficulty of work in such steep and unforgivable terrain, and hazards that ranged from dynamite to marauding grizzly bears, only three men were killed during the construction, one from a fall and two from falling rock.[11]

The Going-to-the-Sun Road rises nearly 3,000 feet in elevation from the McDonald Valley to 6,664 feet at Logan Pass. Grading to the pass was completed on October 20, 1928, and due to the onset of winter weather, automobiles were not allowed to travel to the pass until the next summer.

On the east side of the pass, the road was constructed from St. Mary to Sun Point by 1924. Yet it would not be completed to Logan Pass until 1932. One major obstacle was the East Side Tunnel, which was not holed through until October 19, 1932. The tunnel was 405 feet long—over twice the length of the West Side Tunnel (192 feet long). Grading of the road surface on the east side continued in June 1933, and the entire Going-to-the-Sun Road was opened to automobile traffic on July 11, 1933, four days before the official opening at Logan Pass on July 15. The completed road cost nearly $3 million.

The opening ceremony was a grand affair with nearly 5,000 people attending, including over 150 Indians from the Blackfeet, Flathead, and Kootenai tribes. The Logan Pass parking lot was jam-packed with vehicles, and the Indians set up tepees in surrounding meadows. The present visitor center at Logan Pass was not constructed until 1963–1966, when it was completed as part of the Mission 66 program, a ten-year program initiated in 1956 to upgrade facilities in all the national parks.

Going-to-the-Sun Road was originally a gravel road. Paving began in 1938:

> The route between Belton and Logan Creek became the first section of the road to be paved. Because the park was closed during World War II, the entire length of the Going-to-the-Sun Road was not finally paved until 1952.[12]

Above left: Automobiles on the west side of Going-to-the-Sun Road as witnessed by a Great Northern Railway photographer in 1957. Bird Woman Falls is in the center of the photograph with Mt. Oberlin on the left. (*NPS GLAC10877*)

Above right: Automobiles on the west side of Logan Pass head up Going-to-the-Sun Road, *c.* late 1940s. The cut for the road across the Garden Wall can be seen at upper left center. Logan Pass is in the gap between the Garden Wall on the left and Mt. Oberlin on the right. (*Great Northern Railway photograph, NPS CLAC_11092*)

Below: Going-to-the-Sun Road is newly opened for the season in this George Grant photograph from June 13, 1934 along the Garden Wall. At the top of the wall, the pointed rock formation is known as the "Bishop's Cap." (*NPS GLAC11488*)

Above left: Having crossed Logan Pass, this vehicle and its occupants are headed east down Going-to-the-Sun Road through the "Big Drift," *c.* 1930s. Plowing through this huge snow drift was always one of the largest obstacles to opening the road each season. (*Unknown photographer, NPS GLAC HPF4580*)

Above right: Vehicles head east from Logan Pass on Going-to-the-Sun Road in September 1941. Going-to-the-Sun Mountain is directly ahead. (*Photograph by Marion Post Wolcott, Library of Congress, LC-USF34-058347-D*)

Below: On July 9, 1932, George Grant photographed this automobile and passengers on the Going-to-the-Sun Road at the St. Mary Lake overlook. The East Side Tunnel had not been completed yet, so access to Logan Pass was not yet possible. (*NPS GLAC Grant 0021x*)

In August 1941, Marion Post Wolcott photographed this bend in the Going-to-the-Sun Road high above St. Mary Lake. The curve in the road is the same spot as in the previous George Grant photograph. (*Library of Congress, LC-USF34-058051-D*)

An aerial view of the July 15, 1933, dedication ceremony for the opening of Logan Pass at the summit of the Going-to-the-Sun Road. Hundreds of cars parked on the left, while Indian tepees were set up in the meadow to the right. (*Unknown photographer, NPS GLAC15557a*)

Blackfeet and Flathead Indians dance before throngs of spectators at the opening ceremony for the Going-to-the-Sun Road on July 15, 1933, at Logan Pass. The view is east toward the St. Mary Valley. (*Unknown photographer, NPS GLAC11426*)

Maintenance of the road continues every year, with some years seeing more reconstruction than others. Heavy snowfall, rockslides, waterfalls, and freezing/thawing cycles take a heavy toll on the road each year.

Completion of the Going-to-the-Sun Road had an immediate impact upon the little village of St. Mary on the east side of the park. It was now a major crossroads at the intersection of the Blackfeet Highway and the Going-to-the-Sun Road. Facilities soon sprang up to cater to the needs of the automobile-traveling public:

> In 1932, a former seasonal ranger from Michigan named Hugh Black and his wife Margaret started a small tourist development at the crossroads. They had a small store, six one-room cabins, and an eatery known as the Curly Bear Café.[13]

Over the years, the Black family kept expanding their facilities. In 1952, they built the twenty-seven-room St. Mary Lodge, and they added more rooms to it in 1975, 1989, and 1995. In 2001, they constructed an entirely new hotel to complement St. Mary Lodge—the Great Bear Lodge with forty-eight rooms. In 2011, all the Black family holdings were purchased by Glacier Park Inc.

In 2014, the National Park Service split the hotel concession contract between Glacier Park Inc. and Xanterra Parks and Recreation. Hotels outside the actual Glacier Park boundary (Glacier Park Lodge, St. Mary lodges, and Prince of Wales Hotel) were awarded to Glacier Park Inc. Hotels inside the park (Lake McDonald Lodge, Village Inn at Lake McDonald, and Many Glacier Hotel) were awarded to Xanterra. At the St. Mary facilities today, visitors can purchase gasoline, groceries, sporting goods, and souvenirs; rent hotel rooms or cabins; and eat at the lodge restaurants.

The completion of the Going-to-the-Sun Road was a game-changer:

> [The road] has completely transformed the pattern of travel for Park visitors, making it possible for them to see as much of the peaks and passes in a few hours as might have been encompassed in a week's time by hikers or saddle horse riders.[14]

The road virtually killed the overnight saddle horse tour business and the interior chalets. It offered easy accessibility by automobile to some of the park's most spectacular features and caused an astronomical increase in the number of park visitors from 53,000 in 1932 to nearly 3.3 million in 2017. This crush of visitors has caused huge problems for Glacier National Park today. Reservations are nearly impossible to get at the park campgrounds and hotels. Going-to-the-Sun Road is jammed with vehicles from early morning to sunset. Parking spaces at Logan Pass and other parking areas are constantly filled. As soon as one vehicle pulls out, another one pulls in. Restrooms and garbage facilities are overwhelmed.

George Grant photographed the intersection of the Going-to-the-Sun Road (left) with the Blackfeet Highway (right) at St. Mary on September 12, 1940. The sign at the intersection gives mileage distances to the left (GTS Chalets—10; Logan Pass—18; West Entrance—53) and right (Babb—9; Many Glacier Hotel—20; Waterton Lakes Park—28). The sign at the right of the Blackfeet Highway advertises "Modern Cabins Hugh Black St. Marys." The view is to the north. (*NPS GLAC Grant 1005*)

As Glacier's superintendent stated in 2019, "The very experience people are seeking at Glacier National Park is now being threatened by the sheer numbers of people seeking it."[15] The Park Service is, as of this writing, considering public comments on various strategies proposed to deal with the crowding problems. Whatever the outcome, it is to be hoped that the pristine beauty of the park can be preserved, and the visitor can still experience somewhat of a "wilderness" experience.

Historical Spotlight: Photographer Marion Post Wolcott

Several photographs in this chapter were taken by Marion Post Wolcott. Her photographs of Glacier National Park's scenery are a bit of an anomaly as most of her photographs for the Farm Security Administration documented the plight of rural families in the south during the Great Depression. Her Glacier photographs were taken in August and September 1941, toward the end of her career as a photographer for the Farm Security Administration.

> The purpose of the FSA was to develop solutions to the crises faced by American farmers brought about by drought and the Great Depression. The Historical Section of the FSA, under the leadership of Roy E. Stryker, was created to document, through photographs, the conditions of rural life throughout the country.[16]

Roy Stryker hired Marion Post in 1938. Marion stated:

> As an FSA documentary photographer, I was committed to changing the attitudes of people by familiarizing America with the plight of the underprivileged, especially in rural America ... FSA photographs shocked and aroused public opinion to increase support for the New Deal policies and projects.[17]

Marion was born on June 7, 1910, in New Jersey. Her first career was that of a teacher. In 1932, she traveled to Europe, to study dance at the University of Vienna. While there, she met Trude Fleischmann, a Viennese photographer who encouraged Marion to take up that profession. Nazi activity in Austria soon became dangerous to Marion and Trude, and they came to the United States in 1934. Marion took up teaching and photography. In 1938, she joined the Farm Security Administration as a photographer, carrying out her duties in the south and northeast.

In the latter part of 1940, Roy Stryker assigned her to the western region of the country, and it was during this time period that she took her Glacier photos. In June 1941, she married Leon Wolcott who worked for the U.S. Department of Agriculture. With her new family duties, she soon tired of the constant travel required by her FSA position, and she resigned in February 1942, just a few months after taking her Glacier National Park photographs in August and September 1941.

6

HIKING AND CLIMBING IN THE PARK

From the very beginning, Glacier National Park has always been a hiker's park. The lack of roads in and around the park necessitated the building of trails to connect one side of the park with the other. With Glacier's very limited budget upon the establishment of the park in 1910, it was cheaper to build trails than roads. Also, the Great Northern Railway paid contractors to build trails between its hotels and chalets, the first of which was the Mt. Henry Trail from East Glacier to Two Medicine in 1913. Remarkably, by 1918, most of the major trails in the park had been constructed.

Probably the first organized trail building in what would become Glacier National Park, was the trail built by Dr. Lyman Sperry supervising University of Minnesota students in the building of the trail to Sperry Glacier.

> By 1902, [Sperry] had entered into a unique agreement with Hill whereby the railroad would furnish transportation to and from the area, together with tents, food and supplies, while Sperry would recruit students from the University of Minnesota to do the work without wages for the opportunity of spending a summer in the mountains. The project was started in 1902 and finished by the end of the summer of 1903, the trail being completed to the east side of Gunsight Pass.[1]

Glacier became a national park in 1910.

> Trail building began in earnest, for patrols had to be made, cabins had to be built in the backcountry, and all the valleys and passes had to be traversed by trails in order to increase the efficient administration of the area as well as to allow park visitors to reach the backcountry.[2]

By 1917, 200 miles of trail had been built and the basic trail network had been laid out. In 1921, trails over Stoney Indian and Red Gap passes were completed. Chief Ranger Carter reported in 1930 that 841 miles of trail had been completed or were under construction consisting of—tourist trails: 412 miles; boundary trails: 227 miles; fire trails: 151 miles; and under construction: 51 miles.[3] By 1940, Glacier had nearly 1,000 miles of trails.

Left: Hikers gather for a group photograph at the Sperry basin tent camp in 1911. In 1912, construction of the Sperry Chalets began near here; when completed, the tent camp would no longer be necessary. (*Photograph by Fred Kiser, NPS GLAC7718*)

Below: Hikers have reached the overlook of Sperry Glacier, *c.* 1950, in this photograph by Walt Dyke for the Great Northern Railway. The hike to the glacier is a strenuous 3.5-mile climb from Sperry Chalets with an elevation gain of 1,500 feet. (*NPS GLAC_10802*)

> Glacier's trails have been called its crowning glory. They carry one, afoot or on horseback to the zenith of outdoor enjoyment ... The best of its scenic displays will never be viewed save by those hardy enough to brave the trails.[4]

The National Park Service had assistance building trails in Glacier from Eagle Scouts and Civilian Conservation Corps workers in the 1920s and 1930s. From 1925 to 1931, Eagle Scout Camps were held in the park to help build trails. The scouts were selected from troops throughout the country, and the boys came for twelve-day encampments to build trails. The scouts paid for their transportation to and from Glacier, while the National Park Service paid for their meals, tents, and trail building supplies. The Eagle Scouts helped build trails from Bowman Lake to Brown Pass; the trail to Two Medicine Pass; and the trail along the south shore of St. Mary Lake.

The Civilian Conservation Corps was a Depression-era program established by President Franklin Roosevelt to put unemployed young men to work. "By 1933 there were nine CCC camps in Glacier housing 1,533 officers and men."[5] These young men were "under supervision of Army officers in camp and under civilian foremen and supervisors on the job."[6] Tasks completed by CCC workers included trail building, particularly fire trails and construction of fire lookout towers such as the one on Curly Bear Mountain south of St. Mary Lake completed in 1934.[7] They also installed water and sewer systems, telephone lines, and worked on timber fuels reduction and fire suppression. The CCC operated in Glacier from 1933 to 1942, when it was disbanded due to World War II.

Elmer C. Adams captured the spirit of hiking in Glacier in 1937; he spent twelve days in July in the park hiking 120 miles with members of *The Detroit News* hiking club:

> The Park had been described to us as a hiker's paradise, and, surpassing our expectations, that is what it proved to be. It is not only because nature fitted it for the part, but because it is purposely reserved and developed for the special use of hikers. The railroad and the highways touch only the outer fringe of the area. The whole vast interior with its wealth of beauty and natural phenomena is attainable by none but those who are willing to hoof it or, if they prefer, to ride a horse ... And imagine at intervals of 10 or 15 miles on these trails, so close that one need carry no more than a 10-pound pack, a series of Swiss chalets where, after a day's hike, one may find soft beds, plain but abundant food, and a spirit of simple but hearty hospitality for the night or for as many nights and days as one cares to stay.[8]

Advice on clothing for hikers in 1930s Glacier was given in the *WPA Guide to 1930s Montana*. The writers suggested:

> Shorts are not good for hiking because trails are often closely fringed with bushes. Many hikers wear khaki, but wool is preferable to absorb sweat by day and to give warmth in evening. Stout shoes with thick soles are essential for hiking on rocky trails; [and] should be large enough to enable wearing of two pairs of socks, one thick wool.[9]

In 1949, Park Naturalist George Ruhle gave advice to hikers to "not ruin your trip by attempting too much ... In this rugged country, hikes of 15 miles or more should be attempted only by those who are accustomed to long, hard trips."[10]

Above: One of Glacier's most popular trails is the trail to Grinnell Glacier from the Many Glacier Hotel. George Grant photographed these hikers on July 19, 1932. It is a 10-mile round trip hike, but 4 miles can be cut off by riding the boats across Swiftcurrent and Josephine Lakes. (*NPS GLAC11362*)

Below left: A ranger-led hike to a crevasse on Grinnell Glacier, *c.* 1955. The ranger at left holds an ice ax and one end of a rope, which hikers must stand behind to peer into the crevasse. (*Photograph by Ira Spring for the Great Northern Railway, NPS GLAC_10859*)

Below right: A very early photograph, *c.* 1911, by Fred Kiser shows two hikers/horseback riders at Cracker Lake with Siyeh Mountain in the background. Cracker Lake is a rather grueling 5.6-mile hike from the Many Glacier Hotel, which had not yet been built at the time of this photograph. (*NPS GLAC11242*}

George Grant photographed these hikers at Boulder Glacier on July 27, 1932. Boulder Glacier was reached by trail from Goat Haunt to Brown Pass, a distance of 8.6 miles. It was another 2 miles from the pass to the glacier. Brown Pass could also be reached by the trail from Bowman Lake, which the Eagle Scouts had helped build during their summers in Glacier from 1925–1931. (*NPS GLAC11380*)

Hiking Glacier's trails is still a major attraction for visitors to the park today. The author has hiked many of the most popular trails in Glacier over the past forty years and can attest to the thrill of ascending a pass and viewing the tremendous scenery below; of viewing a mountain goat perched precariously on a ledge overlooking Lake Ellen Wilson; and having a grizzly bear come crashing across the trail in front of him on the Grinnell Glacier Trail. The way to escape the crowds in Glacier National Park today is to head out on the backcountry trails in this glorious place.

Climbing the peaks in Glacier began well before the area became a national park, as early explorers scaled the summits searching for a railroad pass, trail route, or road passageway. Climbing for recreation really did not begin until 1914 when the Seattle Mountaineers held their annual summer outing in Glacier. Their ascent up Mt. Cleveland, the highest mountain in the park at 10,466 feet, was halted by a blizzard on August 11. From 1919 through 1922, "members of the Nature Study Club of Indiana climbed many peaks and left registers in flat metal boxes on Edwards Mountain, Going-to-the-Sun Mountain, Mt. Gould, Mt. Jackson, Mt. Reynolds, Chief Mountain, and Grinnell Mountain."[11] In 1924, the Sierra Club held its annual summer outing in Glacier, climbing several mountains.

In 1926, British climber Dorothy Pilley and her husband I. A. Richards climbed the peaks around Many Glacier guided by Hans Reiss, brother of artist Winold Reiss.

One of Glacier's most scenic trails is the Highline Trail along the Garden Wall from Logan Pass to Granite Park, photographed here by T. J. Hileman, *c*. 1925. It is 7.6 miles from Logan Pass to Granite Park Chalets. (*NPS GLAC8252*)

Dorothy Pilley was born in England in 1893 and at the age of seventeen became a passionate climber, climbing the peaks of Wales and the Alps. In 1926, she married Cambridge Professor Ivor Armstrong (I. A.) Richards, and they continued to climb together throughout their marriage.

Dorothy wrote of Glacier that "some of my best days were experiments to test the attractions of ways over the Divide, from creek to creek, unvisited since the days of the trappers."[12] The rock in Glacier National Park is mainly limestone, a sedimentary rock that breaks and fractures easily. It can be very difficult for climbers to affix pitons to this rock, and when Dorothy Pilley saw Glacier's limestone, she lamented, "Here were the limestone ramparts again ... Limestone is not easy ground to triumph over at sight!"[13] Nevertheless, up she went to dizzying heights captured in photographs by their climbing partner, T. J. Hileman.

With the Great Depression and then World War II, recreational climbing in Glacier did not really begin again until 1947 with the arrival of J. Gordon Edwards. He has been called the "patron saint of climbing in Glacier National Park:"

> [His] love affair with Glacier National park began in the late 1940s when he took a job as a park ranger-naturalist ... Both his wife Alice and daughter Jane have been lifelong climbing companions ... his park service colleagues encouraged Gordon to complete route descriptions. Descriptions first became available as mimeographed sheets at

Above left: An incredible photograph by T. J. Hileman in 1926 shows Dorothy Pilley (below) and I. A. Richards (above) climbing Altyn Peak. The Many Glacier Hotel is below on the left shore of Swiftcurrent Lake with Lake Josephine and Mt. Gould in the distance. Two of the Many Glacier Chalets are at the bottom left, just to the right of the Swiftcurrent Lake spillway. (*NPS GLAC8230*)

Above right: Another remarkable photograph by T. J. Hileman in 1926 shows Hans Reiss, Dorothy Pilley, and I. A. Richards (left to right) climbing Grinnell Point. They are high above Swiftcurrent Lake and the Many Glacier Hotel (bottom right corner). The large lake in the distance is Sherburne. (*NPS GLAC8231*)

Below: This 1926 photograph by T. J. Hileman shows I. A. Richards (left) and Dorothy Pilley (right) perched on the slope of Grinnell Point. Below is Grinnell Lake, and high above it is Grinnell Glacier, clinging to the Garden Wall with Mt. Gould to the left. (*NPS GLAC8230*)

Dorothy Pilley is seen here on the Ptarmigan Wall in 1926 with Elizabeth Lake below. This was prior to the opening of the Ptarmigan Tunnel in 1931. (*Photograph by T. J. Hileman, NPS GLAC8231*)

> ranger stations. Year by year, descriptions grew in number until the [first] climber's guide was published by the Sierra Club [in 1960].[14]

J. Gordon Edwards, from Ohio State University, became a seasonal ranger-naturalist in Glacier in 1947 where he served in the summers through 1956. His *Climber's Guide to Glacier National Park* has been through many editions and publishers since that initial publication by the Sierra Club. It is still the climber's bible for Glacier National Park today. Edwards stated in the introduction to his book:

> Hopefully, this little book will further encourage appreciative men and women to ascend the wild steep slopes and walk the long high ridges of Glacier National Park. Surely an abundance of pleasant memories will then haunt them all the rest of their lives![15]

Denis Twohig, who along with his wife, Shirley, and a group of mountaineering enthusiasts formed the Glacier Mountaineering Society in 1981, also spoke of the allure of climbing in Glacier:

> As a mountain climber I have had the good fortune of pursuing my favorite pastime in this multifaceted world-class mountain region of jagged peaks and towering waterfalls, pristine lakes and glaciers, lush alpine meadows blanketed with colorful wildflowers and being overwhelmed by the panoramas that reveal themselves upon reaching my

> summit destinations. A commonly used term for these eye-popping revelations is Sensory Overload![16]

Climbing in Glacier, though, can always be hazardous. Only experienced climbers should attempt it. Many have died in the pursuit of an elusive summit. Perhaps the greatest climbing tragedy in Glacier was that of the "Mount Cleveland Five" in 1969. Five young men set out to accomplish a winter climb of Glacier's highest peak, Mt. Cleveland, in December 1969. They were attempting a winter climb up the peak's 4,000-foot north face, something that had never been done before. Mt. Cleveland is in the far northern part of Glacier, close to the Canadian border. The young men—James Anderson, Mark Levitan, Clare Pogreba, Jerry Kanzler, and Ray Martin—were transported by boat across Waterton Lake to Goat Haunt on December 27, 1969. They planned to ski and hike from there to Mt. Cleveland. They were due to come out on January 2, 1970. They never made it. A search began for the men on January 3.

> The search ended on January 8. Officials planned to recover the bodies when weather conditions would allow at the start of summer. There were only a few clues ... but all evidence suggested that a large avalanche had engulfed the men in the west bowl near the summit.[17]

On June 29, 1970, the bodies of Ray Martin and James Anderson were found. The bodies of the others were found on July 3. From the west bowl on Mt. Cleveland, the avalanche had swept them down to about 7,500 feet in elevation—a cautionary tale for future climbers, indeed.

The north face of Mt. Cleveland, Glacier National Park's highest peak, is seen in the far distance against the skyline, with Porcupine Ridge off to its right. This photograph, taken from the Bear's Hump in Waterton, Canada, shows Waterton townsite in the foreground and Waterton Lake. (*Photograph by the author, summer 1972*)

HISTORICAL SPOTLIGHT: PHOTOGRAPHER T. J. HILEMAN

The incredible mountain climbing photographs in this chapter were taken by T. J. Hileman. Tomar Jacob Hileman was born in Marienville, PA, on November 6, 1882. He graduated from the Effingham School of Photography in Chicago and moved to Kalispell, MT, in 1911, where he opened a portrait studio. He met Alice Georgeson there, and in 1913, they were married in Glacier National Park at Bridal Falls on McDonald Creek, supposedly the very first wedding in the new national park.

Hileman traveled all over the park taking photographs and he was "an exceptional climber, 'Mountain Goat Hileman' as he was called, often perched precariously on narrow ledges to capture just the right moment on film."[18] The Great Northern Railway hired Hileman as its official photographer in 1925 for $125 a month. Hileman described one climbing expedition in Glacier in 1926:

> I've been out all week with Miss Dorothy Pilley, British mountaineer; Hans Reiss, European guide and artist; and Count Edgar Henckel Domersmaeck of Silesia. Miss Pilley, who is a member of the Ladies Alpine Club ... is spending the summer here to learn whether it might be practical to organize a mountaineer's club.[19]

T. J. Hileman opened photo finishing labs in Many Glacier Hotel and Glacier Park Lodge offering overnight processing of tourists' films. This, along with his postcard reproductions, earned a substantial sum of money, and he was able to build a home on Flathead Lake in 1931. He died there on March 13, 1945.

I. A. Richards and Dorothy Pilley are roped together for safety as they explore a crevasse on a glacier, as witnessed by photographer T. J. Hileman in 1926. The glacier is not identified. (*NPS GLAC8230*)

7

Getting Around Today and Tomorrow

Technological advances have brought all kinds of innovations to transportation equipment in and around Glacier National Park. From double-stack railroad freight cars to incredible highway equipment to airplanes and helicopters, the scene today would have been unimaginable when Glacier became a national park in 1910. We cannot even imagine what transportation will look like in Glacier 100 years from now. Will advances in personal transportation methods relieve the overcrowding on Glacier's roads, parking lots, and trails that is seen today? Will red buses still exist when they are already nearly one hundred years old? Will people still hike trails? Will pandemics such as 2020's COVID-19 decimate the population to the point where people will not even visit Glacier?

As this is being written, Glacier Park Boat Company has canceled their 2020 excursion season, and the red buses have been canceled also. The Blackfeet Tribe has closed visitation to the east side of Glacier for the 2020 tourist season as the highways leading to Two Medicine, Cut Bank, St. Mary, and Many Glacier traverse reservation land. With this pause in heavy visitation, perhaps park officials can develop plans to ease overcrowding for the near future, while awaiting unimaginable technological advances in transportation to come.

Historical Spotlight: Photographer Fred Kiser

Perhaps as we look to the future, it would be beneficial to look back at Glacier National Park's past and remind ourselves of the beauty that existed before development. Photographer Fred Kiser began photographing Glacier even before it became a national park. His photographs are found throughout this book. Kiser was born in Grand Island, Nebraska, in 1878, but it was his parents' move to Warrendale, Oregon, to run the Columbia Beach Hotel that would define his future career.

Fred studied business and commercial law at Portland Business College from 1898–1901, but his real love was photography, which he had been practicing as a hobby with his brother, Oscar. Together, they developed a commercial photography business in 1902 that was immediately successful with their spectacular photographs of the Columbia

Above: A double-stack Burlington Northern Santa Fe freight train passes Glacier Park Station on July 25, 2012. Double-stacked freight containers have revolutionized rail shipping, replacing single-load boxcars and helping divert some truck traffic from the nation's highways. (*Photograph by the author*)

Below left: A snowplow scrapes snow, ice, and rocks from the Going-to-the-Sun Road at the entrance to the West Tunnel on April 4, 2007. (*NPS F4A7FEB8-155D-451F-67AECBF22EA7F9807*)

Below right: On August 8, 2007, an incredible "spider" vehicle is used to rehabilitate guard walls on the Going-to-the-Sun Road above the West Tunnel, which can be seen just a bit left of the green truck. Note the worker at the top of the spider vehicle and the precipitous drop into the valley below. (*NPS F3449B9F-155D-451F-67D637126E5FE582*)

Above left: On October 25, 2007, a road machine is drilling anchor bolts into a rock wall above the Going-to-the-Sun Road. This helps prevent rocks from falling off the wall onto vehicles below. (*NPS F368A4B3-155D-451F-674B3AF202D83DBF*)

Above right: The Robert Fire is burning on the north shore of Lake McDonald in this scene from July 31, 2003. The Canadian-built CL-215 aircraft scoops up water from the lake to drop on the fire. (*NPS CD6471F6-155D-451-F-678383F4948321A6*)

Below: The Robert Fire is still burning in this photograph from August 13, 2003. A Bell 205 helicopter scoops up water from Lake McDonald in the bucket to drop on the fire. (*NPS 40eb8b13-0b02-442a-846f-120616120b2e*)

River Gorge and Crater Lake National Park. Tragically, Oscar drowned in a boating accident in 1905, but Fred carried on, establishing the Kiser Photo Company in Portland.

Fred developed what he called an "Artograph" coloring system for his photographs using oil paints to enhance the photographs. "In 1907, he assembled a touring show of approximately 1,000 of his Artograph scenic views, which traveled to … 20 cities across the country including New York and Chicago."[1] It is likely that Louis Hill of the Great Northern Railway saw this exhibition while searching for a photographer to promote the railway. In 1909, Hill hired Fred Kiser as official photographer for the railway, a contract that lasted for six years.

> His contract with the Great Northern Railway in Montana had the greatest impact on the National Park system … Kiser and his team photographed the spectacular scenery of northwestern Montana, working from headquarters in a specially outfitted railway car provided by the Great Northern. An exhibit of more than 100 of his Artograph prints at the Capitol in Washington, D.C., was credited with providing the final push to gain Congressional approval for establishing Glacier National park in 1910. Kiser marketed his Glacier Park photographs at the Great Northern's tourist facilities for many years.[2]

After Fred Kiser's association with the Great Northern Railway ended, he continued his photographic career at Crater Lake National Park. His business was severely affected by the Great Depression, and he moved to the Los Angeles area where he died in Newport Beach, California in March 1955.

> Kiser's Glacier Park images provided early visual documentation of the Park. He hoped to inspire Americans to preserve their scenic treasures, optimistic that his photos would: 'forever be considered a reminder to future generations … who will exert their strength, their endeavors and their influence exclusively to the conservation of God Given Scenic Beauty for the benefit of posterity.'[3]

Photographer Fred Kiser and his cook are standing next to the special photographic car provided by the Great Northern Railway in the vicinity of Glacier National Park, *c.* 1910. Note the lettering on the car: "Great Northern Photographic Special Car." (*Oregon Historical Society Library, ba021218*)

Endnotes

Introduction

1 Holden, D., quoting the *Kalispell Interlake* newspaper in *Going-To-The-Sun Road 50th Anniversary* (Columbia Falls, MT: The Hungry Horse News, July 15, 1983).
2 Shaw, D. in Guthrie, C., *Glacier National Park the First 100 Years* (Helena, MT: Farcountry Press, 2008), p. vii.
3 Marcus, W., et al., *Atlas of Yellowstone* (Berkeley: University of California Press: 2012), p. 9.
4 *Ibid.*
5 Buchholtz, C., *Man in Glacier* (West Glacier, MT: Glacier Natural History Association, 1993), p. 53.
6 *Ibid.*, p. 56.
7 Alt, D. and Hyndman, D., *Rocks, Ice & Water: The Geology of Waterton-Glacier Park* (Missoula, MT: Mountain Press Publishing Company, 1973), p. 27.
8 Robinson, D., *Through the Years in Glacier National Park* (West Glacier, MT: Glacier Natural History Association, 1960), p. 6.
9 Buchholtz, *op. cit.*, p. 16.
10 *Ibid.*
11 Guthrie, C., *Glacier National Park the First 100 Years* (Helena MT: Farcountry Press, 2008), p. 33.
12 Buchholtz, *op. cit.*, p. 30.
13 Taliaferro, J., *Grinnell: America's Environmental Pioneer and His Restless Drive to Save the West* (New York: Liveright Publishing Corporation, 2019), p. 170.
14 Robinson, D., *Place Names in Glacier National Park* (West Glacier, MT: Glacier Natural History Association, 1963), p. 14.
15 Taliaferro, *op. cit.*, p. 365.
16 Buchholtz, *op. cit.*, p. 47.

Chapter 1

1 Runte, A., *Trains of Discovery* (Niwot, CO: Roberts Rinehart, Inc. Publishers, 1990), p. 31.
2 Quoted in Buchholtz, *Man in Glacier*, p. 46.
3 Guthrie, C., *All Aboard for Glacier: The Great Northern Railway and Glacier National Park* (Helena, MT: Farcountry Press, 2004), p. 9.

4 Yenne, B., *Great Northern Empire Builder* (St. Paul, MN: MBI Publishing Co., 2005), p. 19.
5 Guthrie, *op. cit.*, p.17.
6 Yenne, *op. cit.*, p. 20.
7 Guthrie, *op. cit.*, p. 16.
8 Flandrau, G., *The Story of Marias Pass* (St. Paul, MN: Great Northern Railway, not dated, *c.* late 1920s), p. 5.
9 Yenne, *op. cit.*, p. 24.
10 Guthrie, *op. cit.*, p. 31.
11 Buchholtz, *op. cit.*, p. 38.
12 Guthrie, *op. cit.*, p. 49.
13 Yenne, *op. cit.*, p. 13.
14 Guthrie, *op. cit.*, p. 60.
15 *Ibid.*, p.67.
16 Yenne, *op. cit.*, p. 46.
17 Wood, C., *Lines West* (Burbank, CA: Superior Publishing Co., 1967), p. 56.
18 Dorin, P., *The Domeliners: A Pictorial History of the Penthouse Trains* (Seattle, WA: Superior Publishing Co., 1973), p. 62.
19 Yenne, *op. cit.*, pp. 139–140).
20 Guthrie, *op. cit.*, p. 7.
21 Yenne, *op. cit.*, p. 54.
22 *Ibid.*, p. 59.
23 Tanner, S., *A Biography of Winold Reiss; The Man Who Created the Great Northern Railway's Blackfeet Indian Portraits* (St. Paul, MN: Great Northern Railway Historical Society, June 1996, Reference Sheet No. 242), p. 1.
24 Peterson, L., *The Call of the Mountains: The Artists of Glacier National Park* (Tucson, AZ: Settlers West Galleries, 2002), p. 58.
25 Tanner, *op. cit.*, p. 7.
26 Peterson, *op. cit.*, p. 60.
27 Guthrie, *op. cit.*, p. 76.
28 Read, H. in Linderman, F., *Blackfeet Indians* (New York: Gramercy Books, 1995, reprint of 1935 Great Northern Railway edition), p. 67.

CHAPTER 2

1 Ober, M., *Glacier Album: Historic Photographs of Glacier National Park* (Helena, MT: Riverbend Publishing, 2010), p. 58.
2 Djuff, R., "Glacier on Wheels: Rolling Through the Years" (viad.com/gpibuses.htm: 02/09/2001), p. 2.
3 Ober, *op. cit.*, p. 65.
4 *Ibid.*, p. 60.
5 Djuff, *op. cit.*, p. 3.
6 *Ibid.*
7 Bouda, B., *Jammin'-to-the-Sun: A Tribute to the Red Buses of Glacier National Park* (Kalispell, MT: Digital Broadway Publishing LLC, 2010) p. 7.
8 Djuff, *op. cit.*, p. 7.
9 Glacier Park Foundation Board of Directors. *'Are They History? An Editorial'* (Minneapolis, MN: The Inside Trail Newsletter, Fall, 1999), p. 3.
10 Hagen, J., "Unsung Heroes of the Renovation" (Minneapolis, MN: The Inside Trail Newsletter, Summer, 2002), p. 5.
11 Quoted in Bouda, *op. cit.*, p. 8.
12 *Ibid.*, p. 10.

13 Djuff, R. and Morrison, C., *Glacier's Historic Hotels and Chalets: View With A Room* (Helena, MT: Farcountry Press, 2001), p. 30.
14 Moylan, B., *Glacier's Grandest: A Pictorial History of the Hotels and Chalets of Glacier National Park* (Missoula, MT: Pictorial Histories Publishing Company, Inc., 1995), p. 15.
15 *Ibid.*, p. 43.
16 Hagen, J., *A History of Many Glacier Hotel* (Minneapolis, MN: Glacier Park Foundation, 1985), p. 6.
17 Moylan, *op. cit.* p. 43.
18 Quoted in Djuff and Morrison, *op. cit.*, p. 94.
19 Djuff, R., *High on A Windy Hill: The Story of the Prince of Wales Hotel* (Calgary, AB: Rocky Mountain Books, 1999), p. 22.
20 *Ibid.*, p. 7.
21 *Ibid.*
22 Djuff and Morrison, *op. cit.*, p. 114.
23 Moylan, *op. cit.*, p. 73.
24 Djuff and Morrison, *op. cit.*, p. 139.
25 *Ibid.*, pp. 147–148.

Chapter 3

1 Rinehart, M., *Through Glacier Park In 1915* (Boulder, CO: Roberts Rinehart, Inc. Publishers, 1983, reprint of 1916 original), p. 71.
2 Yenne, B., *Images of America: Glacier National Park* (Charleston, SC: Arcadia Publishing, 2006), p. 31.
3 Robinson, *Through the Years in Glacier National Park*, p.70.
4 *Ibid.*
5 Djuff and Morrison, *Glacier's Historic Hotels and Chalets*, p. 55.
6 Yenne, W., *Switchback: Bill Yenne's 50 Years in the Mountains of Montana and the West* (Kalispell, MT: WY Books, 1983), p. 100.
7 Quoted in Guthrie, *Glacier National Park the First 100 Years*, p. 61.
8 Yenne, W., *op. cit.*, p. 107.
9 Elrod, M., *Elrod's Guide and Book of Information of Glacier National Park* (Missoula, MT: The Missoulian Publishing Co., 1930), p. 211.
10 Quoted in Djuff, R. and Morrison, C. (eds.), *Glacier from The Inside Out: Best Stories From 'The Inside Trail'* (Minneapolis, MN: Glacier Park Foundation, 2012), p. 89.
11 Djuff and Morrison, *op. cit.*, p. 155.
12 Yenne, B., *op. cit.*, p.31.
13 Moylan, B., *Glacier's Grandest*, p. 65.
14 Dunagan, B., *Welcome to Sperry Chalet* (Whitefish, MT: Beth Dunagan, 2013), pp. 111–112.
15 Hagen, J., "Wild Fire In Glacier and Waterton" (Minneapolis, MN: The Inside Trail Newsletter, Fall, 2017), p.3.
16 Djuff and Morrison, *op. cit.*, p. 107.

Chapter 4

1 Hackethorn, J., '*Glacier National Park Boats*' (Washington, DC: National Register of Historic Places, nps.gov/nr/feature/places/pdfs/AD_64501275_11_14_2016.pdf), p.12.
2 *Ibid.*, pp. 12–13.
3 Robinson, *Through the Years in Glacier National Park*, p. 75.
4 Hackethorn, *op. cit.*, p. 14.

5 Djuff, R., *The Prince of Wales Hotel* (Waterton Park, AB: Waterton Natural History Association, 1991), p. 36.
6 Robinson, *op. cit.*, p. 76.
7 Hackethorn, *op. cit.*, p. 13.
8 Robinson, *op. cit.*, p. 75.
9 Hackethorn, *op. cit.*, p. 19.
10 Hagen, J., "*Boat Concession Up for Bids*," (Minneapolis, MN: The Inside Trail Newsletter, Spring 2019), p. 3.
11 Davis, R. and Davis, H., *Landscapes for the People: George Alexander Grant, First Chief Photographer of the National Park Service* (Athens: University of Georgia Press, 2015), p. 62.
12 McFarland, G. (Introduction), *Trains, Trails, & Tin Lizzies: Glacier National Park 1932–1934, Photographic Plates from the George A. Grant Collection* (West Glacier, MT: Glacier Natural History Association, 1987), unpaginated.

Chapter 5

1 Robinson, *Through the Years in Glacier National Park, op. cit.*, p. 86.
2 *Ibid.*, p. 87.
3 Morrison, C., *Chief Mountain International Highway: Waterton-Glacier's Promised Road* (Waterton Park, AB: Goathaunt Publishing, 2010), p. 45.
4 *Ibid.*, p. 92.
5 Goble, F., *The 20 Cent Men* (Cardston, AB: Goble Publishing Limited, 2000) p. 3.
6 Morrison, *op. cit.*, p. 87.
7 Hanna, W., *Montana's Many-Splendored Glacierland* (Seattle, WA: Superior Publishing, 1976), p. 126.
8 *Ibid.*, p. 123.
9 Ruhle, G., *Guide to Glacier National Park* (Minneapolis, MN: John W. Forney, 1963), p. 27.
10 Houk, R., *Going-To-The-Sun: The Story of the Highway Across Glacier National Park* (Del Mar, CA: Woodlands Press, 1984), p. 16.
11 Yenne, B., *Images of America: Going-To-The-Sun Road* (Charleston, SC: Arcadia Publishing, 2013), p. 17.
12 *Ibid.* p. 39.
13 Yenne, *Images of America: Glacier National Park, op. cit.*, p. 92.
14 Hanna, *op. cit.*, p. 128.
15 "*Managing the Crush: Park Service Proposes New Plan for Managing Glacier's Crowds,*" (Great Falls, MT: Great Falls Tribune, September 30, 2019).
16 Butler, M., *Images of America: High Road to Taos* (Charleston, SC: Arcadia Publishing, 2016), p. 8.
17 Quoted in Wolcott-Moore, L., "*A Biographical Sketch of Marion Post Wolcott.*" (people.virginia.edu/~ds8s/mpw/mpw-bio.html)

Chapter 6

1 Hanna, *Montana's Many-Splendored Glacierland*, p. 119.
2 Robinson, *Through the Years in Glacier National Park*, p. 94.
3 Elrod, *Elrod's Guide and Book of Information of Glacier National Park*, p. 30.
4 Hanna, *op. cit.*, p. 117.
5 Ober, *Glacier Album*, p. 25.
6 Robinson, *op. cit.*, p. 98.
7 Butler, D., *Images of America: Fire Lookouts of Glacier National Park* (Charleston, SC: Arcadia Publishing, 2014), p. 71.

8 Quoted in Pederson, H., *E Che Kar: An Unforgettable Hike Through Glacier National Park In 1937 and the History of the Park* (Green Valley, AZ: Henry F. Pederson, Jr., 2003), p. 85.
9 Federal Writer's Project, *The WPA Guide to 1930s Montana* (Tucson: University of Arizona Press, 1994), p. 376.
10 Ruhle, *Guide to Glacier National Park*, p. 20.
11 Edwards, J., *A Climber's Guide to Glacier National Park* (West Glacier, MT: Glacier Natural History Association, 1990), p. 40.
12 Pilley, D., *Climbing Days* (London: The Hogarth Press, 1989, reprint of 1935 edition), pp. 297–298.
13 *Ibid.*
14 Larson, R. in Edwards, J., *op. cit.*, p. 7
15 Edwards, *op. cit.*, p. 18.
16 Twohig, D. (Foreword) in Passmore, B., *Up on the Roof: Views from Glacier's High Places* (Kalispell, MT: Montana Outdoor Guidebooks, 2014), unpaginated.
17 Guthrie, C., and Fagre, D. and A., *Death & Survival in Glacier National Park* (Helena, MT: Farcountry Press, 2017), p. 184.
18 Peterson, *The Call of the Mountains*, pp. 50–53.
19 *Ibid.*

Chapter 7

1 Oregon Historical Society. "Fred Kiser Biographical Note," (archiveswest.orbiscascade.org/ark:/80444/xv22241)
2 *Ibid.*
3 Quoted in Peterson, *The Call of the Mountains*, p. 40.

BIBLIOGRAPHY

Alt, D. and Hyndman, D., *Rocks, Ice & Water: The Geology of Waterton-Glacier Parks* (Missoula, MT: Mountain Press Publishing Company, 1973)

Atkinson, G. and Atkinson, J., *Izaak Walton Inn: A History of the Izaak Walton Inn and Essex, Montana* (Columbia Falls, MT: Hungry Horse News, 1985)

Bouda, B., *Jammin'-To-The-Sun: A Tribute to the Red Buses of Glacier National Park* (Kalispell, MT: Digital Broadway Publishing, LLC, 2010); *The Era of the Chalets 1914–2014* (Kalispell, MT: Digital Broadway Publishing, LLC, 2014)

Buchholtz, C., *Man in Glacier* (West Glacier, MT: Glacier Natural History Association, 1993)

Butler, D., *Images of America: Fire Lookouts of Glacier National Park* (Charleston, SC: Arcadia Publishing, 2014)

Butler, M., *Images of America: High Road to Taos* (Charleston, SC: Arcadia Publishing, 2016)

Davis, R. and Davis, H., *Landscapes for the People: George Alexander Grant, First Chief Photographer of the National Park Service* (Athens: University of Georgia Press, 2015)

Djuff, R., *The Prince of Wales Hotel* (Waterton Park, AB: Waterton Natural History Association, 1991); *High on A Windy Hill: The Story of the Prince of Wales Hotel* (Calgary, AB: Rocky Mountain Books, 1999); *'Glacier On Wheels: Rolling Through the Years'* (viad.com/gpibuses.htm:02/09/2001)

Djuff, R. and Morrison, C., *Glacier's Historic Hotels and Chalets: View with A Room* (Helena, MT: Farcountry Press, 2001); *Glacier From The Inside Out: Best Stories From The 'Inside Trail'* (Minneapolis, MN: Glacier Park Foundation, 2012)

Dorin, P., *The Domeliners: A Pictorial history of the Penthouse Trains* (Seattle, WA: Superior Publishing, 1973)

Dunagan, B., *Welcome to Sperry Chalet* (Whitefish, MT: Beth Dunagan, 2013)

Editor. *'Managing the Crush: Park Service Proposes New Plan for Managing Glacier's Crowds'* (Great Falls, MT: Great Falls Tribune, September 30, 2019)

Edwards, J., *A Climber's Guide to Glacier National Park* (West Glacier, MT: Glacier Natural History Association, 1990)

Elrod, M., *Elrod's Guide and Book of Information of Glacier National Park* (Missoula, MT: The Missoulian Publishing Company, 1930)

Federal Writer's Project, *The WPA Guide to 1930s Montana* (Tucson: University of Arizona Press, 1994)

Glacier Park Foundation Board of Directors, *Are They History? An Editorial* (Minneapolis, MN: The Inside Trail Newsletter, Summer, 2002)

Goble, F., *The 20 Cent Men* (Cardston, AB: Goble Publishing Limited, 2000)

Guthrie, C., *Glacier National Park the First 100 Years* (Helena, MT: Farcountry Press, 2008);

All Aboard for Glacier: The Great Northern Railway and Glacier National Park (Helena, MT: Farcountry Press, 2004)

Guthrie, C., and Fagre, D. and A., *Death & Survival in Glacier National Park* (Helena, MT: Farcountry Press, 2017)

Hackethorn, J., *'Glacier National Park Boats'* (Washington, DC: National Register of Historic Places, nps.gov/nr/feature/places/pdfs/AD_64501275_11_14_2016.pdf)

Hagen, J., *A History of Many Glacier Hotel* (Minneapolis, MN: Glacier Park Foundation, 1985); *'Unsung Heroes of the Renovation'* (Minneapolis, MN: The Inside Trail Newsletter, Summer, 2002); *'Wildfire In Glacier and Waterton'* (Minneapolis, MN: The Inside Trail Newsletter, Fall, 2017); *'Boat Concession Up For Bids'* (Minneapolis, MN: The Inside Trail Newsletter, Spring, 2019)

Hanna, W., *Montana's Many-Splendored Glacierland* (Seattle, WA: Superior Publishing, 1976)

Holden, D., *Going-to-the-Sun Road 50th Anniversary* (Columbia Falls, MT: The Hungry Horse News, July 15, 1983)

Holterman, J., *Place Names of Glacier/Waterton National Parks* (West Glacier, MT: Glacier Natural History Association, 1985)

Houk, R., *Going-to-the-Sun: The Story of the Highway Across Glacier National Park* (Del Mar, CA: Woodlands Press, 1984)

Kennedy, T., *In Search of the Mount Cleveland Five* (Bozeman, MT: Bridger Ridge Rewriters Guild, 2017)

Larson, R. (Foreward) in Edwards, J., *A Climber's Guide to Glacier National Park* (West Glacier, MT: Glacier Natural History Association, 1990)

Marcus, W., et al., *Atlas of Yellowstone* (Berkeley: University of California Press, 2012)

McFarland, G. (Introduction), *Trains, Trails & Tin Lizzies: Glacier National Park 1932–1934, Photographic Plates from the George A. Grant Collection* (West Glacier, MT: Glacier Natural History Association, 1987)

Morrison, C., *Chief Mountain International Highway: Waterton-Glacier's Promised Road* (Waterton Park, AB: Goathaunt Publishing, 2010)

Moylan, B., *Glacier's Grandest: A Pictorial History of the Hotels and Chalets of Glacier National Park* (Missoula, MT: Pictorial Histories Publishing Company, Inc., 1995)

Ober, M., *Glacier Album: Historic Photographs of Glacier National Park* (Helena, MT: Riverbend Publishing, 2010)

Oregon Historical Society, *Fred Kiser Biographical Note* (archiveswest.orbiscascade.org/ark:/80444/xv22241)

Pederson, H., *E Che Kar: An Unforgettable Hike Through Glacier National Park in 1937 and the History of the Park* (Green Valley, AZ: Henry F. Pederson, Jr., 2003)

Peterson, L., *The Call of the Mountains: The Artists of Glacier National Park* (Tucson, AZ: Settlers West Galleries, 2002)

Pilley, D., *Climbing Days* (London: The Hogarth Press, 1989)

Read, H. in Linderman, F., *Blackfeet Indians* (New York: Gramercy Books, 1995)

Rinehart, M., *Through Glacier Park in 1915* (Boulder, CO: Roberts Rinehart, Inc., Publishers, 1983)

Robinson, D., *Through the Years in Glacier National Park* (West Glacier, MT: Glacier Natural History Association, 1960); *Place Names in Glacier National Park* (West Glacier, MT: Glacier Natural History Association, 1963)

Ruhle, G., *Guide to Glacier National Park* (Minneapolis, MN: John W. Forney, 1963)

Runte, A., *Trains of Discovery* (Niwot, CO: Roberts Rinehart, Inc., Publishers, 1990)

Shaw, D., in Guthrie, C., *Glacier National Park the First 100 Years* (Helena, MT: Farcountry Press, 2008)

Taliaferro, J., *Grinnell: America's Environmental Pioneer and His Restless Drive to Save the West* (New York: Liveright Publishing Corporation, 2019)

Tanner, S., *A Biography of Winold Reiss: The Man Who Created the Great Northern Railway's Blackfeet Indian Portraits* (St. Paul, MN: Great Northern Railway Historical Society, 1996)

Twohig, D., (Foreword) in Passmore, B. *Up on the Roof: Views from Glacier's High Places* (Kalispell, MT: Montana Outdoor Guidebooks, 2014)

Wolcott-Moore, L., *A Biographical Sketch of Marion Post Wolcott* (people.virginia.edu/~ds85/mpw/mpw-bio.html)

Wood, C., *Lines West* (Burbank, CA: Superior Publishing Company, 1967)

Yenne, B., *Great Northern Empire Builder* (St. Paul, MN: MBI Publishing Co., 2005); *Images of America: Glacier National Park* (Charleston, SC: Arcadia Publishing, 2006); *Images of America: Going-To-The-Sun Road* (Charleston, SC: Arcadia Publishing, 2013)

Yenne, W., *Switchback: Bill Yenne's 50 Years in the Mountains of Montana and the West* (Kalispell, MT: WY Books, 1983)